stuck!

navigating the transitions of life & leadership

TERRY B. WALLING

Revised Edition

© Terry Walling

First edition published 2008

Revised edition published 2015

Leader Breakthru

Resourcing and coaching breakthrough in the lives
of risk-taking, Kingdom leaders.

www.leaderbreakthru.com

P.O. Box 463, Chico, CA USA 95926

dedication

I wrote the first edition of this book back in 2008 to resource the many leaders I was coaching at the time who found themselves in the in-between of life and leadership called a "transition." Since its release, hundreds more have been helped by the ability to identify and better understand the transition moments we each must face. I've been overwhelmed by the response of so many who have shared the breakthroughs they experienced from *Stuck!*

This updated edition remains true to its original purpose of clearly and concisely describing a transition and God's shaping purposes.

I'm deeply grateful to Elliott Haught for his editorial help and to Kyle and Megan Walling for their graphic design and formatting work on this book.

I'm deeply thankful for my mentor, Dr. J. Robert Clinton and the impact he's had on my life. His research in the area of leadership development and his personal mentoring and coaching have resulted in breakthrough moments in my own development as a leader. His generosity and empowerment to take his research and make it user-friendly has left an indelible mark on my life and ministry.

I dedicate this book to the following four people who have walked alongside my life, nurtured my life, and have believed in me through many transition moments. Their unending love and support has made all the difference.

- For *Robin*, because you believed in me when I didn't believe in myself and because you have loved me so well.

- For *Donya*, because your life has transitioned into one who nurtures the lives of God's special gifts so well.

- For *Kyle*, because God has transitioned your life into one who is passionate to see an authentic life in Christ and a Church that matches the truth it is founded upon.

- For *Brianna*, because you have transitioned into a leader who has focus and abilities only surpassed by your caring heart.

contents

PART 4: TRANSITIONS — LEARNING & RESPONDING

Appendix

Resources—LEADER BREAKTHRU

foreword: *Dr. J. Robert Clinton*

Over a lifetime, as Christ-followers and leaders continue to grow and mature, they will experience distinct phases of development. As leaders move from one level of development to the next, often involving a new phase, they will face a period involving a transition.

Many folks do not weather transitions very well and so appear to be stuck. They need to move on, through the transition, to the next level of development in their lives. Terry Walling deals with this "boundary" time in this book. But he also deals with other transitions—the tough times that also occur in the middle of a development phase. Hence, the title, *Stuck!*

Terry has organized this teaching on transitions into four parts. Each of these parts gives important information that can help you get "unstuck" and move you through your transition.

Part 1: Transitions—Defined gives an overall perspective of what a transition is. It warns against trying to hurry up and take a shortcut through the transition. The important thing to remember from this warning is that you want to get all that God has for you out of the transition before moving on from it. Knowing why transitions occur will help you process them more fruitfully.

Terry offers some underlying reasons for why transitions are needed. And, finally, he closes Part 1 with an overview of a transition, which involves a four-phase cycle: (1) Entry, (2) Evaluation, (3) Alignment, and (4) Direction. By the time you finish Part I, you will have a good overview of transitions and will be ready to plow through the next three parts, which give detailed help about moving through the four-phase cycle.

In Part 2, he guides you through processing the details of this cycle. Terry gives characteristics of each of the four phases in the cycle. Forewarned is forearmed! In the Entry Phase, Terry warns that you will have confusion. But you will get through it and be able to evaluate what is happening to you. He then describes two fundamental attributes of the Alignment Phase. As you work through alignment, your direction will clarify. In fact, you will begin to sense God moving you to your destiny.

Part 2 will help you analyze your own unique transition.

Part 3 is about defining moments. Terry gives comparative information about the three general transitions you will face. All leaders typically go through these three kinds of general transitions. Terry then points out the important role coaching plays as you work your way through these transitions. I am particularly interested in chapter 16, which deals with legacy, since that is where I presently am.

Finally, in Part 4, Terry looks at Transitions—Learning and Responding. He gives several pieces of advice to help you get the most out of your transition. Knowing these will help you better interpret and work through what God intends for you during this time.

The strength of Terry's work lies in its encouragement to your heart during your transition. A transition is a normal thing. All Christ-followers and leaders go through them. Terry uses many illustrations to reinforce the fact that you are not the only one going through this challenging, yet important season.

Stuck! will help you get "unstuck" as you face tough times in your life and as God is promoting you on to the next phase or chapters of your development.

Blessings as you get "unstuck,"

Dr. J. Robert Clinton
Author of *The Making of a Leader* and numerous
leadership development resources
September 2008

preface

We were lost.

I was six years old. My sister was four. We were wandering in circles in a forest near our suburban home outside of Hartford, Connecticut. To this day, I vividly remember a growing desperation inside my young heart, *Are we ever going to find our way out of all this?*

"Terry, are we lost?" my sister asked, nervously. "I want to go home. When are we going to get home? We're going to find Mommy, aren't we?"

I did my best to reassure her, but I wasn't at all sure myself.

We had been sledding in this area many times. So much so that Mom thought we could find our way back. On this day, our playmates had left for home without us. The recent snowfall had blurred our familiar route. The longer I tried to lead us out, the more confused I became. Even at my young age, I remember beginning to entertain the thought that we might not find our way home.

And then, there it was. Through the clearing, I could see the outline of our house. I could see the way out and the path to get there. Never did home look so good.

No matter what age a person is, being lost is not something anyone enjoys. You crave the familiar, something to help you gain your bearings.

You may be in a role in which you must act as if you know where you're going, even when you know you're nothing but lost.

Christ-followers can get lost in their journeys with God. They arrive at moments when what worked before no longer works for them now. God's voice that seemed so loud and clear in the past now seems to have grown strangely quiet and distant.

During these defining moments, some return to what's familiar and, in doing so, miss the God-intended growth. Some wander off, confused by all the questions of what's next. Some plateau in their faith. Some walk away. Some make it through.

Transitions occur in the lives of all committed Christ-followers. They are the moments and days that lie between what is and what is to come. Transitions are the seam between one development phase and the next.

They deepen one's trust and dependency on God and help Christ-followers acquire greater voice recognition of God's voice. *Stuck!* is about finding God in new ways and discovering His purposes, while at the same time trying to survive and navigate a time of transition.

WHAT'S AHEAD?

- The definition of a transition

- How to know if you're in a transition

- How transitions occur and a generic pathway for a transition

- How God uses a transition to shape a Christ-follower's life and direction

- The keys to navigating the important and hard moments of a transition

- How to know when a transition ends, and what you can expect in the future

You most likely picked up this book because you are in—or close to—a time of transition. When you're in a transition, you don't need new theories or speculations about what God "might" be doing. What you need is a guide! You need information and a guide to help walk you through. *Stuck!* seeks to offer both.

Ahead is a paradigm and framework to help you better understand what occurs during a transition and process the confusion you may be experiencing. The following pages will offer a series of interpretive helps through which to organize your questions and hang your emotions. You'll be introduced to coaching tips that can help you process all that is occurring as you move from one stage of your development to the next.

You'll also be introduced to the Transition Life Cycle, a road map to help you recognize where you are in your transition, as well as what lies ahead. Finally, *Stuck!* will introduce you to the three major transitions all Christ-followers face and offer insights into what to expect during each of them.

Over the past 30 years of ministry, I've listened to the stories of hundreds of leaders and committed Christ-followers. Together, we've walked them through the apparent confusion that can come from a transition and that sense of being "stuck" in their life and development. We've been able to uncover insights that apply to all leaders and Christ-followers, as well as the deep yearnings that have remained trapped in their own hearts for years.

Over and over again, I've witnessed how transitions play a major role in moving committed Christ-followers from where they are to where they need to be. God uses transitions to unfold His sovereign purposes. They are part of how the future will unfold in their lives. Your transitions will do the same for you.

Be aware, however! Many of those I've coached have walked along the edge of quitting. In these times, I've watched God deliver a break-through—even in the impossible. Over and over, I've seen God speak hope and destiny to even the most discouraged leader and Christ-follow-er. Few if any of these were able to navigate a transition alone. We were designed to walk together.

I've been fortunate to have a mentor who has walked me through many of my life and leadership transitions. Dr. J. Robert Clinton has done extensive research into lifelong leadership development and how God shapes leaders. He served as Professor of Leadership Development at Fuller Theological Seminary for over 40 years. He studied over 5,000 his-torical, biblical, and contemporary leaders. His insights about transitions (he uses the term boundaries) and his mentoring in my life have given me the courage to keep walking, especially into unknown and unwanted places. I'm deeply grateful for him, and I pass on what I have learned through him and others to you.

The early chapters of *Stuck!* will define a transition, introduce you to a generic pattern for how transitions typically evolve (the Transition Life Cycle)—along with providing some navigational tools to help you better identify how to make it through—and help you consider how God might be at work during a transition.

Next, we'll look at the three major transitions that all Christ-followers go through en route to living out one's calling and destiny. Each of these transitions has a unique purpose and goal. Each of these transitions helps to surface the unique contribution of people like you.

In the final chapters, I'll describe ways one can approach a transition, along with reasons not to quit early on this challenging time. In order to live out the life God has intended for each of us, we will need transitions to get there. The ability to finish well requires times in life where we pause, listen to God, and learn lessons and values that we'll need in the future.

HOPE

There is good news, however, even with all the challenges that come with a transition: new hope comes as a result. And hope brings with it new courage to face old challenges.

Transitions take time, but they also come to an end. The key to transitions is to gain all you can from them. Get all of what God has from the time in between because it will end and then you'll need that deeper trust and that greater clarity in order to go to the new places ahead of you.

The more you know about transitions, the more you can join God in His work. The more you align yourself with His work, the more you will see where He is leading you in the future. And the more you see how God is at work in your life, the greater your potential will be to finish your life even more passionate about and committed to Christ as when you began.

In one of the darkest moments of Israel's history, God gave His people a promise. This promise likely isn't new to your ears, but it needs to be personally applied to our lives, like it was to a people lost and living in captivity. "I know the plans I have for you," declares the Lord, "plans to give you a future and a hope" (Jeremiah 29:11). These words ring true today for us.

Even when you feel confusion surrounding you, and when God seems to be working opposite of all you know about Him, don't give up. You can make it through. God is still at work and He knows what He is doing.

Knowing about transitions can help you live your life with a greater sense of destiny and purpose, but you need to want to.

My encouragement to you, then, is simple: want to.

Terry Walling
Chico, CA
February 2015

Author's Note: Please take time to read the Summary section on the next few pages. It will help set the stage for you as you seek to better understand transitions.

summary

Stuck! focuses on the life and leadership transitions that each of us will face. Christians and non-Christians alike have discussed the need to better navigate life and leadership transitions. What is new in the pages of *Stuck!*, however, is a deeper understanding of how God uses transitions to shape the destiny and character of a Christ-follower. Ahead, you'll discover that God does some of His most important work in the lives of His followers during the in-between times of a transition.

It is the desire of most every Christ-follower to hear the words, "Well done, good and faithful servant!" (Matthew 25:21) at the end of his or her life. The problem is that even committed Christ-followers can get lost en route to hearing those words. Many have become paralyzed by difficult life experiences. Many of these moments occur during the transition from one phase of personal development to the next.

Difficult moments or experiences can often be used by God to signal the beginning of a new work or stage in one's development. God uses these defining moments in ways not often apparent. Failure to navigate these formation moments has contributed to men and women, like you and I, shrinking back from God's best.

The purpose and goal of this book is two-fold. First, it seeks to empower passionate Christ-followers and leaders with the tools necessary to work through a time of transition, gaining all of what God intends. Second, it seeks to counteract the potential stagnation that often results from a transition. Through being able to identify and align with God's greater purpose during transition moments, I hope that many more Christ followers hear the words, "Well done."

DEFINITIONS

This book must be read with some definitions in mind. These terms provide the key frameworks surrounding the concepts of life and leadership transitions.

First—and most basic—what is a transition?

A *transition* is a defined period of time where one phase or period of an individual's development ends and another phase or period needs to begin. A transition represents that in-between time. Transitions move a Christ-follower from somewhere to somewhere else.

Transitions (or personal development boundaries) are well documented in the leadership development study and research of Dr. J. Robert Clinton of Fuller Theological Seminary. His writings undergird many of the insights found in *Stuck!*. I've taken Clinton's work and added my own insights based on 30 years of coaching leaders. Transitions play an important role in the development of leaders and committed Christ-followers.

MAJOR TRANSITIONS

Transitions serve to bring about needed change, provide clarity in life direction, consolidate learning, deepen values, shift paradigms, and advance one's influence and/or ministry.

There are three important transitions that occur in the personal development of committed and passionate Christ-followers. These major transitions move one toward greater influence and growth, helping to shape a life for a unique and ultimate contribution, whether one works and ministers in a vocational ministry role or lives and serves Christ in the marketplace.

These three generic transitions are:

- The Awakening Transition (often occurring in one's 20s or 30s)

- The Deciding Transition (often occurring in one's 40s or 50s)

- The Finishing Transition (often occurring one's 60s or 70s)

MICRO TRANSITIONS

Other transitions exist, however—ones different than the in-between moments of the three major transitions. These occur along the way, often within a larger phase of one's development so that he or she continues to grow. These are known as *micro-transitions* or sub-phase transitions and they move a follower from one sub-phase of his or her development to another.

Finishing well is a term that refers to reaching the end of one's life and having been faithful to the calling God has placed on that life. Finishing well is about Christ-followers being more passionate about Christ and His mission as they fulfill their life purpose than they were in the beginning. It also entails a life that experiences the depth of God's grace and love.

An individual who finishes well is more surrendered to God's will and desires and more focused on running the race to the end. It's the living out of one's destiny and the making of one's unique and ultimate contribution in the expanding of God's Kingdom.

The word "mindset" is defined as (1) a fixed mental attitude or disposition that predetermines a person's response to, and interpretations of, situations or (2) an inclination or habit.

A *sovereign mindset* is the key intentional choice that allows an individual to see life and its circumstances with developmental eyes. This predisposition that God has always been at work brings ongoing insight about God and His purposes.

Paradigm shifts are often the by-product of a transition. Paradigm shifts are the change of one's perspective, attitude, approach, and/or understanding of a given circumstance or set of facts. In a paradigm shift, an individual or group learns to process the same information and facts in new ways. Paradigm shifts provide new ideas and ways to overcome old obstacles. Transitions often initiate shifts in a Christ-follower's perspective and paradigm.

Paradigm shifts break unhealthy behavior patterns, leading to new approaches to life and leadership. Without transitions, and the paradigm shifts that occur with them, Christ-followers would stay stuck! The ability to look at the same facts in new ways and see new truths releases a Christ-follower and leader to a new level of influence.

Faith Challenges are defining moments when a Christ-follower must decide to put "weight" on the new direction and life decisions that a transition can produce. God tests the dependency and trust of His followers by calling them to take new steps and move beyond current levels of growth and capacity. Rest-assured that as transitions unfold, they will call for new faith as one moves into the future.

THE PATHWAY OF A TRANSITION

Transitions often travel down a generic pathway. This pathway consists of four steps or phases of a transition: the Entry Phase, the Evaluation Phase, the Alignment Phase, and the Direction Phase. Each phase plays a role in moving a Christ-follower from a time of isolation to a new hunger for God's plan to the time of processing of obstacles and roadblocks (often issues of pain and wounding) to discovering the new way forward.

In the Entry Phase, a follower often experiences a time of isolation or conflict that launches a deeper search for God and a hunger for clarity.

In the Evaluation Phase, a follower begins to assess what has transpired, what God is seeking to reveal, and the convictions and lessons that need to be brought into future decision-making.

In the Alignment Phase, there's often a time of surrender as a follower comes face-to-face with issues of brokenness, inadequacy, and renewed submission to God's purpose and desires. The prize of this time of surrender is a fresh revelation of God's desired future.

In the Direction Phase, the future and a sense of destiny surfaces. Confusion, which once seemed unending, finally lifts and new experiences begin to point the way forward. As followers take new steps of faith, they move on to the next chapter in their life and development.

The majority of the time in a transition is spent in evaluation and surrender. As a Christ-follower captures lessons from the past, Christ begins to unfold the future. Sometimes, the only thing tougher than not knowing where one is going is knowing and realizing that the future will require new steps of faith and trust in God.

Whether Christ-followers focus their time and efforts on their business, their family, their local church, or their community or government, these same principles apply.

God uses transitions to shape life direction and further the discovery of one's unique contribution in the expansion of His Kingdom.

END RESULT

Convergence is the focused time when a Christ-follower reaches the end, only to discover a unique contribution: the net result of years of formation and life experience. Convergence involves the coming together of "who" God has shaped an individual to be and a sense of "for this I was born." Transitions are one of the key tools that move a Christ-follower along that journey. Christ-followers move from an individualized life and purpose to leaving behind a legacy for others.

Transitions also:

- Break Christ-followers free
- Move a Christ-follower from somewhere to somewhere else
- Surface greater clarity in God's call on a Christ-follower's life
- Clarify a Christ-follower's unique role
- Call for focus and greater intentionality
- Are catalysts in a Christ follower's life purpose
- Produce greater self-definition and discovery of how to influence others to live out God's purposes

HOW TO READ THIS BOOK

Stuck! should be read and used according to where you are in your own journey. If you want to better understand transitions, read the chapters of this book in order. However, if you sense that you're in a time of transition, then you need perspective and insight now. If that's you, using the overview below, skip to the chapters most applicable to your current life situation. Below is a description of the flow of the book.

THE EARLY CHAPTERS

In chapters 1–4, the focus is on better defining transitions and identifying the characteristics and key reasons behind them. Go to these chapters to determine if you're currently experiencing a transition and to help you better define and identify the nature of a transition.

Chapters 5–10 introduce the Transition Life Cycle and the pathway of a typical transition. The Transition Life Cycle will provide a map, helping give greater clarity to the actual steps through a transition. Go to these chapters to better understand where you might be in your transition and what to expect in the future.

THE MIDDLE CHAPTERS

In chapters 11–16, we'll take a closer look at the three major transitions every Christ-follower will face. There's a good chance that you picked up this book because you're in one of these three transitions, each of which has a unique purpose and goal.

There are two chapters for each of the three transitions: one chapter describing it and the next chapter offering coaching help. Go to the one that most closely approximates your current stage of development. Then, double back to the chapters describing the other two major transitions.

THE FINAL CHAPTERS

In chapters 17–20, I explain why you shouldn't quit your transition early. These chapters provide tangible helps that describe what God does during a transition and how to best approach the transitions you face.

Go to these chapters if you're feeling restless in your transition and if you need to re-think how to approach transitions in the future.

ADDITIONAL RESOURCES

At the end of each chapter, you'll find links to the Leader Breakthru website and additional resources to help you gain greater clarity during your time of transition.

Appendix A is a discussion guide to use *Stuck!* in a small group context.

Appendix B provides excerpts from the seminal research by Dr. J. Robert Clinton, and his major article related to transitions, "Boundary Processing."

Appendix C offers more information about Leader Breakthru and the coaching and resourcing you may need in the days ahead.

1

real life

So much of this life is lived in between, between the now and the not yet, between arriving and departing, between growing up and growing old, between questions and answers. Lord, help us not to live for the distant day when the in-between will be no more, but help us to have the courage to step into that sacred space of the in-between—knowing that this is a place where life is transformed.

—JIM BRANCH, *THE BLUE BOOK*

Every transition begins with an ending. We have to let go of the old thing before we can pick up the new— not just outwardly, but inwardly.

—WILLIAM BRIDGES, *MANAGING TRANSITIONS*

The defining moment recounted below is true. It's the story of an actual Christ-follower who lives and is committed to please His God. He thought he knew what God wanted him to do—and then *it* happened.

"Terry, you've got to help me out! Something's all wrong! I don't know what's happening."

"Okay, slow down" I responded. "Tell me what's up, Daniel. What's going on?"

"I don't know what's going on! That's the point. I don't know if I'm confused, depressed, lazy, or all three. Am I losing it? I don't know where I am anymore, and I have no clue where I'm going."

"What brought all of this on?" I asked. "I know things have been tough, but the last time we talked, you seemed to feel like you were on track."

"I know," he replied. "But now I wonder if I've been off for some time now. No matter what I try, nothing seems to get any better. And worst of all, God has gone silent. I thought I was doing what God wanted me to, but I feel like I've completely lost the plot."

"Slow down," I responded, as calmly as possible. "And let's walk our way back through this together. It sounds like there's more going on here than just a bad week!"

Daniel and I then proceeded to walk back through his past and then forward through months of fog and uncertainty that had clearly descended on his life. Step by step, we trudged through self-doubt, questions of adequacy, and fears that somehow he had gotten things wrong in terms of knowing what God wanted.

The real problem wasn't that Daniel had gotten it wrong, but, rather, the more he tried to sort it all out, the more his paralysis spread. Every door he tried to pry open to help answer his confusion proved to be yet another dead end. Daniel was stuck.

Daniel and his wife are among the best and most gifted Christ-followers I know. Long ago, they had surrendered their lives to the control of Jesus Christ and they had followed their King to the front lines of Christian ministry. Somehow, we can let ourselves get trapped into thinking that our best and brightest are beyond these moments of feeling lost. But that's not true.

No matter how mature one may be as a Christian, a person can only handle so much frustration, confusion, and lack of direction before he or she begins to lose hope. Daniel had done all the right things, yet answers from God seemed to move further and further away. I was beginning to hear and feel a loss of resolve seeping into his voice as we continued our coaching relationship over the phone. Behind him was a place where he knew he couldn't return to in his spiritual growth, but ahead of him was a path for the next chapter with God that was both unknown and uncertain.

Daniel was on a pilgrimage of character that all Christ-followers must face from time to time. It was much more than merely a period of frustration or things not going his way. Instead, Daniel had entered a defining moment in his development as a leader and Christ follower called a transition. Without exception, every committed Christ-follower and leader will be called to travel this same road.

But, as he traveled, Daniel had hit a danger moment in his transition. The endless loop of frustration and confusion had taken its toll. He was close to the edge of losing the new ministry God had for him. From the outside, I could see a trap was being set. His weariness and confusion were being used by the enemy to lure Daniel away from all that God was intending to do within him. Like so many before him, Daniel wanted an easy fix or a shortcut to a deeper, true work of God.

Many committed Christ-followers have jumped off-road as a result of times like these. Short-circuited transitions have led to times of plateau, arrested development, and even walking away from the faith.

Who doesn't want to fast-forward to the good stuff? Who doesn't want hope more than confusion and to live in victory as opposed to apparent failure? However noble we may each look on the outside, we've all flirted with how we might quietly skip the hard stuff.

Our many books and workshops often serve to fuel those shortcut desires. Type A individuals are especially at risk. They typically want to "cut to the chase," get to the finish line, and forgo the mess of wandering deeper into the processing fog. Whatever your personality type, we all hit those moments when enough is enough.

Transitions occur in the lives of business people, vocational ministers, homemakers, students, young and old, church and non-churched alike. For Christ-followers, something more is occurring—something more than just a change in career direction or the need for new scenery. God does some of His most important formation during the transition times of His followers. He sculpts life purpose and direction during the in-between times of our lives.

Transitions aren't new. Transitions pushed Moses onward, moving him beyond his doubts and inadequacies. A major transition occurred in Joshua's life that thrust him into a major role of leadership, taking the Israelites into the Promise Land. It was a series of life transitions that transformed a fisherman named Peter into an apostolic leader of the early church.

Transitions were also used to advance the lives and leadership roles of Bonhoeffer, Wesley, and Moody, along with more contemporary figures like Graham, Bright, and Warren. Each of those who have gone before us have experienced major times of in-between: times full of uncertainty and questions en route to living lives that please God.

Transitions are also occurring in the lives of people like you and me. They happen every day among faithful followers of Jesus: moms, kids, friends, brothers and sisters, work associates, and more all experience transitions. God uses transitions to both deepen and widen the influence of those who choose to love Christ with their lives.

It was nearly two years later when I received a phone message from Daniel. The recorded cell phone update was short, clear, and enthusiastic:

"Hey, Walling! I've had a breakthrough. I see what's next and what God is at work doing! Don't coach me any more about this in-between, transition stuff. God is speaking again! Hallelujah! Call me if you want to know more. If not, just get out of my way! I'm movin' out. See ya!"

ROSIE AND MARTIN

On April 21, 1980, Rosie Ruiz crossed the finish line as the first female finisher in the 84th Boston Marathon—and in record time. Or did she? Race officials determined later that she had not completed the entire 26.2-mile course. Instead, she had registered for the race, joined the other runners near the end, and sprinted to the finish line as the apparent winner.

No one had actually seen her running in the race. She didn't appear in any of the videotape footage. Members of the crowd only reported seeing her enter the race in the last mile. Her time of 2:31:56 was an unusual improvement of more than 25 minutes ahead of her "reported time" in the New York City Marathon, just six months earlier.

In 2001, New York City Marathon race officials posted a fifth-place finish for Martin Franklin. The problem, however, was that Franklin ran only the start and finish of the race. At the start, he stood proudly on the Verrazano Bridge. The gun went off and he started the race, along with the other runners.

Franklin had obviously studied his profession. His approach to winning the marathon was the same as Rosie Ruiz's in 1980. He began the race, but then left the race to take the subway. Franklin had a history of cheating in races. Apparently, he showed up in earlier races portraying himself as an elite runner and athlete. He did so at the Green Bay Marathon, the Vermont City Marathon, and the San Diego Marathon. He was awarded $200 at the Green Bay Marathon for his "finishing" time in the race.

Franklin was spotted by riders on the nearby subway. He exited at Eighth Avenue. He was seen heading toward the finish line wearing his championship spandex uniform. The observers joked that he must be doing some serious cheating. Franklin did not let their words deter him.

A few minutes later, these same observers were shocked to see Mr. Franklin making his final sprint to the finish.

Race officials challenged Franklin after the race, but he remained insistent that he had run the entire distance, regardless of what the witnesses had said. Franklin was next spotted skipping town. Who knows where he is today? He might be on a subway somewhere, riding with Rosie.

ARE YOU STUCK?

Are you running the race, yet caught in an endless loop of uncertainty? Do you need answers now, but none seem forthcoming? Or do you remember a time like this in your journey as a Christ-follower? Or maybe your instincts are telling you that a moment like this looms on the horizon.

You wouldn't be the first to want to skip ahead, to take a quick subway ride to the finish line. Applause, for all of us, feels so much better than isolation and despair. No one likes being stuck. Everyone is prone to want to shortcut a transition to get onto greater spiritual growth. Don't do it. It's vital for you to get all you can out of the transitions you face.

Instead, draw encouragement and courage from the truth that all Christ-followers go through times of transition. In the end, transitions produce the new clarity and hope you crave. Transition moments are defining moments that perform an important personal development purpose. The more you know and learn God's purposes in the midst of transitions, the more you can join Him in His shaping of your life.

UNSTUCK: APPLYING IT

In this first chapter, we established the reality that transition moments occur in the lives of all Christ-followers, even the most passionate and committed.

In the next chapter, we'll define and describe transitions in greater detail. Chapter 2 will also explain some of the reasons why a Christ-follower must go through a series of transitions in his or her life.

Before going on, stop and reflect for a moment:

- Describe what you've felt during the last few months.

- List some key words that seem to characterize what's going on right now.

- What's happening between you and God?

- Do you have a sense that there's something more going on? If so, what?

- Spend time journaling your thoughts before going to the next chapter.

2

different

We spend most of our lives trying to make things happen for our-selves, and for the people we love. But life cannot be reduced to what you give or know or achieve. Life is not reduced to your mis-takes, your failures, or your sin. Life isn't even defined by whom you love. Rather, it is defined by the God who loves you.

—M. CRAIG BARNES, *SACRED THIRST*

...until Christ is formed in you.

—GALATIANS 4:19

ccess stories abound. Men and women who are victorious in
? paraded in front of those struggling and hungry for some-
ent. It's almost impossible to not be tempted, and even envi-
ther person's success and breakthroughs. And although many
try to make sure that we don't copy their methods, we do it anyway, be-
lieving that their answers can become our own.

The issue is that the apparent success is misleading. Hidden from us
are the in-between moments of confusion and transition that drive a
Christ-follower deeper into the heart of God. Times of isolation, restlessness, conflict, and deep inner struggles will be used by God to produce
different kinds of lives and ministries. Transitions are often the defining
moments where godly character is forged.

God imparts His presence and authority to those who will allow Him to
work them through times of transition. Kingdom influence is the by-product
of men and women who allow God to do a deeper work in their lives.

As darkness descends on a post-Christian western culture, Christ-
followers need to know about personal and organizational transitions
now more than ever. The days ahead will be different than any we've
faced before. The days and times are ripe with change. These moments
often catalyze personal transitions

The question remains: Will we stay on the surface and try to copy
someone else's methods, or will we allow God to transition each of our
walks with Him to a new place? This chapter will help better define a
transition and bring to the surface its characteristics.

WHAT IS A TRANSITION?

A transition is an in-between period in the life development of a
Christ-follower. In a transition, individuals consolidate past learning,
process issues of character, deepen convictions and values, and are
prepared for the next phase of their development. Transitions bring
closure to the past in order to move forward to the next stage of personal development.

Transitions are characterized by a prolonged period of restlessness,
self-doubt, lack of motivation, stagnation, diminished confidence, lack of
direction, distance from God, isolation, relational conflict and tension,
lack of effectiveness, and a struggle to stay focused and motivated.

You may currently feel some of these traits on a regular basis. But with a transition, characteristics like these persist over a prolonged period of time.

Another way to recognize a transition is the realization of the deeper work that God is doing. Transitions are more about character development than job description. In a transition, God turns a searchlight on the heart.

Transitions are often filled with far more questions than answers—questions such as:

- Why have I lost my passion?

- Why can't I shake this restlessness?

- Why do I feel isolated?

- Why all the inconsistencies?

- Why do I keep rehearsing tapes from the past?

- What would happen if I do step out?

- What if I fail?

In the midst of all these questions, it's important to keep in mind some truths about transitions, including:

- Transitions take time, often from three months to three years.

- They are common to every Christ-follower.

- They often involve revisiting difficult moments and struggles.

- They are often intensified when a Christ-follower is also leading others.

- They are a major tool used by God to shape character and life direction.

- They come to an end.

We crave certainty, but God desires to give His followers clarity. Transitions often bring clarity to Christ-followers on three fronts: self-definition, role, and new paradigms. Let's explore each of these.

SELF-DEFINITION

God uses transitions to help followers press into greater clarity about who they are. Self-knowledge is essential for emotional health and for coming to terms with one's unique contribution. God uses transitions to help Christ-followers discover who they are, but also who they aren't. For these reasons, transitions often include struggles with self-confidence, relational tensions with family and friends, feelings of self-worth and a lack of acceptance, and struggles with fear and personal inadequacy.

ROLE

Role is about more than one's job. Role has to do with contribution. Over a lifetime, God desires to bring to the surface the good works that He has authored for all Christ-followers (Ephesians 2:10). Each person is gifted to make an impact. Transitions bring clarity to the working together of one's abilities, skills, and spiritual gifts. Role clarifies contribution in the church, on the job, and in your family and community. For these reasons, transitions often include ongoing frustrations over effectiveness, continued struggle with job fit, and restlessness over passion and contribution. A hunger grows to not just live a life of busy work.

PARADIGMS

Transitions also bring to the surface the need for new knowledge and necessary changes in one's paradigms. In order to move forward, each Christ-follower needs to think in new ways, as well as achieve greater clarity in one's knowledge base. Lifelong learning is one key to finishing well. A breakthrough in worldview often comes with new opportunities and options. For these reasons, transitions often include challenges to one's presuppositions, disturb plateaus in growth, bring to the surface the need for education and training, and create an internal restlessness for a deeper journey with God.

DIFFERENT

Almost every person I know describes their life with God as going differently than they expected or planned. The unexpected surprises even the faithful. Life often becomes too planned and ordered, so God intervenes and the different begins to happen. Somewhere, different becomes the destination and something different becomes the desired end-result. Different is often born out of the transition moments in one's journey.

Going through transitions is about God having the right to be God. Transitions forge new trust. Without transitions, we would slide into a malaise of the same and stop growing. Because of this, God allows the difficult, the confusing, and even the hurtful to enter a life—not because of His lack of caring, but to take us deeper into our pursuit of Him.

What makes this issue of greater relevance and impact today is the unprecedented, global change that now drives life into a time of perpetual transition. The speed of change is throwing fuel upon the intensity already present in transitions.

What's really around the bend? We need to admit to ourselves that we don't know. None of us is really quite sure what lies ahead. At best, we're defining what will be (post-modernity) by what it is not (modernity). One thing is clear, though: life has changed and it will be different than the one most of us have known and found comfort in. The formula-driven Christianity and three or five simple steps we studied in the past won't work for today or tomorrow.

The future must be forged from a realization that we live in a different land, are a part of a different world, and need a different kind of faith—one built upon the reality of change and a deeper intimacy with Christ. But, to get there, it'll take the courage to go to a different place, be a different kind of Church, and walk a different path—a path a transition can produce.

UN-STUCK: APPLYING IT

Processing your transitions. Knowing yourself. Living differently. Most do little in terms of thinking about their development. Most struggle with seeing God's purposes in current circumstances.

Think of a time of transition in your life. Retrieve it from your memory. What happened? What was different about yourself as a result?

In this chapter, we defined the characteristics of a transition and discussed the benefits that Christ-followers gain from transitions.

In the next chapter, we'll discuss the role that transitions play in the lifelong development of Christ-followers.

3

why?

All journeys are similar; all journeys are different

—JANET HAGBERG, *THE CRITICAL JOURNEY*

As long as I am plagued by doubts about my self worth, I keep looking for gratification from people around me. But when I can slowly detach myself from this need for human affirmation, and discover that it is in relationship with Jesus that I find my true self.

—HENRI NOUWEN, *THE GENESEE DIARY*

Questions that have driven many parents crazy, that have seeded many teenagers' rebellions, and that have been refrains in the lives of many emerging young adults are also the same questions that surface at some point during any transition:

- Why do things have to change?

- Why is God allowing all of this to happen?

- Why is He silent when I need answers?

- Why has the future disappeared?

- Where is all of this heading?

The vast majority of the people who purchased *The Purpose-Driven Life* by Rick Warren were Christians—Christians hungering for direction and meaning. It's one thing to know that your life has purpose; it's another to know what that purpose is.

God uses transitions to better align people's lives with His purposes. Transitions propel a life forward by creating a pause in one's current life path. They provide a way to capture lessons from the past that are needed to clarify purpose and direction. Transitions help address the question, "Why?"

STEWARDING

All over the world, I've taken an informal poll. I've asked Christ-followers this simple question: "What do you want to hear from our Lord at the end of your lives?"

Overwhelmingly, the answer has been the same, no matter the age, gender, or culture: "Well done, good and faithful servant" (Matthew 25:21). All Christ-followers want to know that their lives have counted.

They want to know that they have pleased God.

My next question, then, is this: "Where is that statement found in the Bible?" In a group, someone typically breaks the silence by reminding the group that it comes from the parable of the talents in Matthew 25:14-30.

Each parable has one central truth. The parable of the talents is about stewardship: God entrusts to each believer experiences, abilities, skills, and giftedness. He calls us to intentionally invest our lives in the extension of Christ's kingdom as an act of stewardship and worship.

Transitions are about stewardship, about the re-investment of these life deposits. The pause created by a transition gives time to process lessons, reexamine pain and wounding, and gain perspective on God's purposes. God also uses transitions to begin unveiling pieces of our legacies.

Transitions are also about helping Christ-followers move beyond their current struggles and fears. Important choices can be made based on the stewardship of life's lessons and experiences.

DEVELOPMENT

God develops each of us over a lifetime. Because of this, we'll go through a series of chapters or phases in our development. We'll face moments of plateau and stagnation in our spiritual growth and development. Transitions often provide a holy "kick in the pants." They move Christ-followers beyond their current stage by creating a hunger and desire for more.

Transitions build bridges to what's next.

Many have written about the stages of a life and the transitions through which we pass. Janet Hagberg's *The Critical Journey* describes six stages of growth and a major transition she calls "The Wall," where the Christian journey turns inward.

William Bridges has written some important books on transitions (*Transitions: Making Sense of Life's Changes* and *Jobshift*). In these books, he defines transitions from a non-Christian point of view. He provides strategies for coping with transitions and the role they play in a life. Bridges enables readers to understand that transitions help both in identifying and in coping with critical changes in our lives.

Dr. J. Robert Clinton has studied how God develops leaders. In *The Making of a Leader*, he outlines a set of six generic phases. His research has uncovered the role transitions play in keeping leaders and Christ-followers on track and moving forward in their development. On the following page is a diagram that displays Dr. Clinton's stages of development as portrayed in a generalized timeline.

Each of our developments move from one stage to another as we journey with Christ. The word development means "unfolding." Transitions move a Christ-follower from one phase of personal growth and development to the next.

Your pilgrimage with Christ will move from your initial experience with God (Inner Life Growth), to the beginning of your serving of God (Ministry Maturing), and into a time where God uses life itself and its complexity (Life Maturing) to deepen your walk with Him. As life continues to unfold, transitions move a Christ-follower along.

Every phase of one's development has a purpose. Failing to process the challenges and implications of each phase can mean moving to the next one with unfinished business dragging behind. Whenever we enter a time of transition, old issues from the past can reemerge. Often, these issues can be traced back to questions about God, His plans, and, often, His lack of presence in our lives.

Rarely are we honest about how little control we have over life. Rarer still do we process questions regarding the faithfulness of God. Yet, the questions still exist and each stage of development brings new ones.

David surfaced his questioning with songs. They reflected the cry of his heart: "Will the Lord reject forever? Will he never show his favor again? Has his unfailing love vanished forever? Has his promise failed for all time? Has God forgotten to be merciful? Has he in anger withheld his compassion? Then I thought, 'To this I will appeal'" (Psalm 77:7-10).

WHY TRANSITIONS?

Why do transitions occur? Here's another thought.

Those who have been in the Church for many years may recall a particular children's song that had hand motions and repetitious verses:

Deep and wide,
Deep and wide,
There's a fountain flowing deep and wide.
Deep and wide,
Deep and wide,
There's a fountain flowing deep and wide.

I believe this simple children's song is profound. Look again at the words. How does the fountain flow? The presence of God flows first deep, then wide. Our ability to live for God is directly linked to our dependency and intimacy with God.

It's in transitions that we often grapple with the deeper issues and learn that effective lives for God flow from being. God grants greater influence and increased spiritual authority to those who courageously choose to go deep with Christ. God uses those who lean into pain and issues from their past, as opposed to living in denial.

This diagram shows how this works.

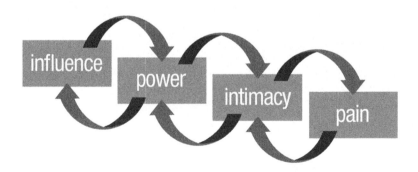

This diagram (also known as the Influence Continuum) reveals that influence for Christ is the by-product of deeper healing and intimacy with Christ. As a result of God's work in our lives, we experience new freedom and resolution past issues that often hold us back and God grants to us a greater measure of his favor and expanded influence.

UN-STUCK: APPLYING IT

Understanding why a transition is occurring is often only possible when you look back. Try to answer these questions about a current or recent transition:

- Why did God choose to push the pause button on your journey?

- What is it that He might be trying to address? Add? Affirm? Adjust?

- Why did God choose the timing He did? Why now?

In this chapter, we discussed the role that transitions play in our life-long development and the stewarding of life experiences that God brings into our lives.

In the next chapter, we'll unpack the generic pathway that transitions often take as they unfold in the development of a Christ-follower and leader.

4

the life cycle

*My starting point is that we're already there. We cannot attain the
presence of God because we're totally in the presence of God.
What's absent is our awareness.*

—RICHARD ROHR, *EVERYTHING BELONGS*

*This experience can be gradual or radical. It can take place
through everyday events, or in an extraordinary experience. It can
be one focal event, or a whole sequence that finally falls together.*

—ROBERT MULHOLLAND JR., *INVITATION TO A JOURNEY*

There's a way through a transition. You can gain an understanding of where you are and what lies ahead. Knowing where you are is often the key to knowing where you're going.

The Transition Life Cycle (introduced below) provides a generic snapshot of a transition. It has been derived from examining many lives that have gone through a transition.

If you're experiencing a transition, you'll find yourself somewhere on the Transition Life Cycle. Determining where you are in your transition provides navigational coordinates to help you better move into the future. It also calls on you to stay the course. The more you stay the course, the more you learn to trust God. The more you know that God can be trusted now, the more you will trust Him in the future.

A transition typically progresses through four phases, culminating in a Faith Challenge. Note the following diagram:

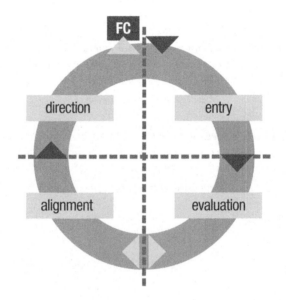

AN OVERVIEW OF TRANSITIONS

Before we take an in-depth look at how a transition typically unfolds, let's gain an overview of a transition as a whole. Following is a summary of the four phases.

Entry into a transition often goes unrecognized. In the beginning of a transition, individuals often just struggle to cope with the challenges, confusion, struggles, or conflict that surround a transition.

The Entry Phase of a transition is often characterized by emotions of restlessness, confusion, self-doubt, and isolation, as well as relational trauma and a consistent lack of energy. Life situations unravel. Life crisis and relational conflicts happen. Mounting uncertainty and persistent problems create the need for perspective.

The continuing agitation of not being able to "make life work" leads to a realization that something very different is occurring: a transition. It also becomes evident that some type of evaluation is needed. This first phase then moves into a time of evaluation.

The Evaluation Phase of a transition causes a Christ-follower to look back. In this evaluation, Christ-followers often rehearse past struggles, confront issues of wounding, consolidate lessons, deepen convictions, and challenge life assumptions. Evaluation is accelerated and deepened when one can externalize his or her thoughts and reflection. Evaluation and alignment with God's will often work together. As a Christ-follower better understands the past, needs for prayer and surrender can surface.

The Alignment Phase is embodied by the act of surrendering to God's sovereign will and agenda. Alignment causes Christ-followers to become more pliable, teachable, open-minded, and open-hearted to needed change. Often, God must confront people with strong egos, those who pride themselves with being self-sufficient, and those with issues related to hurt from others, issues of shame and guilt over secret sin, or issues that surface of which they were previously unaware.

Alignment isn't just about repentance. Christ followers also may need to accept God's grace and deep, enduring love in greater ways. Busy doers and those who focus hard on tasks must face themselves—sometimes for the first time—and experience God in new ways. This would have not occurred if not for a transition.

Beyond alignment and surrender is the Direction Phase. The breakthrough moment in a transition comes as a follower moves from alignment to direction. This can come in an unexpected conversation, a throwaway line, or at the edges of a new thought.

Destiny experiences then begin to occur. These experiences are part of the destiny processing in this phase. Destiny Revelation is the moment when God reveals new direction for the future. As a Christ-follower begins to act on what God has revealed, destiny fulfillment occurs.

The end of transition brings a Christ-follower to a crossroads of faith. A Faith Challenge relates to a Christ-follower putting faith in the new course direction and stepping out in obedience.

You will face many transitions in your life. Getting all you can from them will help facilitate the journey of Christ-followers finishing well. The characteristics of a transition (chapter 2) and the concept of the Transition Life Cycle help to demystify the process of a transition.

Understanding what a transition looks like is helpful. Applying the concepts of the Transition Life Cycle to your own transition can provide you with interpretive breakthroughs. The more you can apply the Transition Life Cycle, the more you gain insights into how God is at work, even during times of uncertainty and confusion.

UN-STUCK: APPLYING IT

As you read this chapter, did you feel like you're in a transition?

- If so, where do you think you are in the cycle?

- What has God been saying to you?

- What issues seem to be surfacing?

- What's been your response?

In the following chapters, we'll explore each phase of the Transition Life Cycle in greater detail.

In this chapter, we mapped out the life cycle of a transition. The four phases reveal both the work God does, as well as what a Christ-follower can expect as he or she progresses through a transition.

In the next chapter, we'll dive deeper into the Entry Phase of a transition and will work to understand how God initiates this new season.

5

confusion

Never once did it occur to me that when I found the trail again, it would ruin my life forever. For once you feel the breath of God breathe on your skins, you can never turn back, you can never settle for what was, you can only move recklessly, with abandon, your heart filled with fear and your ears ringing with those constant words, "Fear Not."

—MIKE YACONELLI

Lord, I know I am rigid. I have been pretending and hiding for a long time. I am afraid of you, and of being out of control of my life. I am coming out of the hiding. These things are true: I have shaped my life to make myself look good. I have lived my existence around myself, not you. I continually resist your transformation of my life. I am tired of resisting you.

—TERRY WALLING

She's a seasoned Christ-follower. Having served in vocational ministry for several years, she now teaches the Bible to those hungry for more. Her passion has been to mentor many into a deeper walk with Christ.

In the past, through times of challenge and struggle, God had met her, offering answers and assurance. She cherished His sufficiency and provision. His ways and plans continued to unfold as she followed Christ deeper into His Word. That was the pattern for many years. Until one day, it stopped.

Her pattern for listening to God and hearing God's voice seemed to come to an abrupt halt. It started with a series of crisis moments.

The loss of two children through miscarriages, the struggle with the foster care system, the denial of an adoption, struggles with past family issues, and the near loss of a soulmate all did her in. And as if that weren't enough, her ministry opportunities ran dry.

Separately, each of the situations she faced was difficult. Together, they were overwhelming. As she reached out to God for comfort and help, He seemed strangely quiet. No reassurance. No sense of His presence. Nothing. She sank deeper and deeper into isolation. The aloneness began closing in.

In the past, she'd been quick to defend God and His character in times like she was now experiencing. But this time, she sank deeper into quietness. She was committed to remain. She wasn't going to walk away from her faith, but God's silence left many more questions than answers.

It truly was an unusual place for her. This communicator, whose teaching and counsel had brought clarity to so many others, was now at a loss for words regarding her own life.

One thing was clear, though: this wasn't going away any time soon. She was in a different place in her journey with God. Having exhausted all of her known options, she was in a new period of her journey. She had entered a transition.

TRANSITION ENTRY SYMPTOMS

It's not unusual for a Christ-follower to experience something similar to this teacher's experience—to wake up one day and discover the reality of a transition. Clarity on what it all means will come later. But, at first, confusion reigns. Transitions often launch with traumatic life experiences. They serve to catapult an individual into a time of isolation, questioning, and struggle.

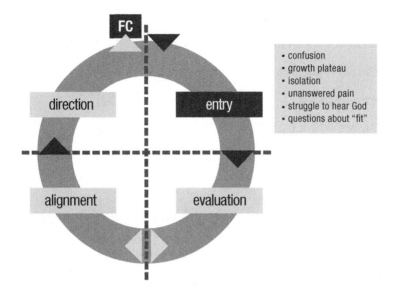

- confusion
- growth plateau
- isolation
- unanswered pain
- struggle to hear God
- questions about "fit"

Today's overcommitted schedules and the compartmentalizing of life serve to intensify these emotions. A busy mom, seeking to maintain a high level of ministry involvement and facing the mounting struggles of life, is similar to other stories being played out in other life situations. Silence—and even apparent indifference—from God reveals that something different has begun.

Chapter 4 briefly describes the entry into a transition. Entering into a transition can be further characterized by the loss of motivation and energy, self-doubt, and a struggle to make life work. These will not go away. The more a Christ-follower seeks to bring resolution, the worse it gets.

Life crisis situations can often signal the entry into a transition. This includes relational conflict, loss of friendships, marriage or family struggles, friction in the workplace, job loss, and a loss of personal vision. As the struggles continue, isolation grows. Even the most committed Christ-followers begin to know that they need some type of breakthrough. Hope and courage are linked. As hope diminishes, so does courage. They begin to be replaced by anger and despair.

Here's an entry checklist. Three or more positive responses indicate that you may be entering a transition:

- Persistent restlessness

- Isolation, even in the midst of a crowd

- Internal confusion

- External conflict

- Hunger to hear from God, yet He is silent

- Inability to move forward or change the situation

How'd you do?

The entry stage of a transition is about letting go. Often, God is calling our pretending into question. God will no longer allow His followers to hide behind the false story they've constructed about the world and their view of themselves.

This entry into a transition is actually a familiar road. It closely approximates what Christian experienced in John Bunyan's *The Pilgrim's Progress*. In his journey, it's called the "unread road." This journey is full of unknown answers and unknown challenges. It's difficult to undertake a journey like this without guidance from past experience, a road map, or someone to help guide us through.

There are ways to recognize how God works during the entry point of a transition. Each of these processing agents is designed to break the normal patterns of lifestyle and to challenge current behaviors. They are sculpting tools in the hands of the Potter who has already begun shaping and re-shaping the Christ-follower.

ISOLATION

Isolation Processing refers to those events or circumstances that cause an individual to feel set aside—separated from those things and people that once brought life. Isolation is about a disengagement from the normal activities that often surround life and ministry. It doesn't mean that a Christ-follower has stopped working and functioning as a person. Rather, there's a loss of connection with all that is occurring around him or her. Isolation creates this dark sense of aloneness. It can make a Christ-follower ripe for spiritual attack and oppression.

The isolation that is part of the Entry Phase of a transition rarely means that a Christ-follower is being removed from serving God. Many times, he or she is busy and very active in working with others. However, he or she begins to do it in a "bubble" of being isolated from people and typical results. This isolation creates the need for evaluation. It also produces a deeper hunger for God and a desperation that previously was not felt.

Biblical Example: Jacob became isolated and alone as he battled God for answers to his prayer (Genesis 32:22-32).

LIFE CRISES

The entry into a transition can also occur through a series of processing events known as Life Crises. Life Crises encompass a wide array of events or circumstances, but each involves a growing sense of pressure, turmoil, and difficulty, often building to a fear that what is occurring is insurmountable. Life Crises can include issues of security, health, finances, hurts, changes in life stage, family trauma, marital conflict, loss of employment, and relational tension with others.

The pressure of Life Crises processing is often compounded because the struggles seem to multiply and occur simultaneously. Handled separately, each of these situations would be difficult, but together they compound fears and doubts among even the strongest believers. These Life Crises can often deliver a near-fatal blow to the emotional and spiritual strength of even the most devout Christ-followers. Life Crises create desperation for God and His intervention.

Biblical Example: Job faced apparent rejections by God, his friends, and his wife. Each of these crisis moments seems to be compounded as Job's testing progresses (Job 4:3-4, 7-8; 8:20; 11:14-15,17).

CONFLICT PROCESSING

As is already apparent, there's overlap between several of these processing items, but Conflict Processing often occurs in the Entry Phase of a transition. Interpersonal struggles seem to heat up, often with no apparent reason. Conflict and relational struggles often occur between work associates, ministry partners, family members, or close friends. These conflicts can be over values, methodologies, personalities, philosophies, or personal preferences. Whereas in the past things seemed settled, now little seems the same.

Conflict is the reality of life with others. The purpose of the tension is to pinpoint and identify needed areas of growth and change. In a transition, God often uses conflict to initiate a time of questioning and reevaluation. Conflict Processing places a Christ-follower in a state of being out of control—one main reason why people try to avoid conflict. Yet, it's here that God often moves in, using times of conflict to create deeper trust and dependency on Him.

Biblical Examples: Paul and Barnabas's disagreement over John-Mark resulted in a time of separation. Also, the early church had relational conflicts and problems. God used these conflicts to shape these individuals and the Church (Acts 15:36-41).

NEGATIVE PREPARATION

Negative Preparation is a processing moment often difficult to understand. It can involve struggles with business partners, close friends, or ministry associates. The issues or failures of another can hurt a Christ-follower.

However, Negative Preparation can also break a Christ-follower free to move on to the next chapter in his or her development.

The choices of another can thwart your opportunities, diminish your ability to exercise your gifts and demonstrate leadership, or stifle your ability to actualize your potential. Often, the greatest hurts and struggles come from those closest to us.

Negative Preparation can send a Christ-follower in search of answers. It often occurs at the front end of a transition and frees a follower to consider heading in a new direction.

Biblical Example: Joseph was betrayed and shamed by his own brothers. They clearly intended to harm him. But God took their acts of jealousy (Genesis 37) and evil toward Joseph and worked them together for good (Genesis 50:20).

UN-STUCK: APPLYING IT

What if you realize that you're at the Entry Phase of a transition? What should you do?

- Adopt a posture of openness. Instead of seeking to end or remedy your struggles, open up to what God might be doing in your life.

- Start a journal. Write down your thoughts about where you are. List the issues that you find yourself pondering. What are your questions?

- Reflect on the issues that you believe launched you into the transition. What's the nature of those issues? Why are they so difficult?

- Ask God to begin to reveal His purposes, even in the midst of your hurt and confusion. Pray and reflect by asking, "Lord, what are you at work doing?"

- Find someone to travel alongside you. This shouldn't be someone who claims to have all the answers, but someone committed to helping you process your questions.

- Wait. If you're truly in a time of transition, it will unfold.

In this chapter, we saw how transitions can begin unnoticed to a leader or Christ-follower. God often uses times of isolation, conflict, and negative events to launch a transition.

In the next chapter, we'll look at the next phase of a transition. We refer to it as "living under the waterline" because this transition moves into a time of evaluation and alignment.

6

waterline

The word detachment might evoke the wrong impressions. It aims at correcting one's own anxious grasping in order to free oneself for a committed relationship with God.

—JOHN ELDREDGE, *THE JOURNEY OF DESIRE*

Jesus invites us to embrace our brokenness as he embraced the cross, and live it as part of our mission. He asks us not to reject our brokenness as a curse from God that reminds us of our sinfulness, but to accept it and put it under God's blessing for our purification and sanctification. Thus our brokenness can become a gateway to new life.

—HENRI NOUWEN, *BREAD FOR THE JOURNEY*

Several years ago, Eugene Peterson, author of *The Message*, wrote a book called *A Long Obedience in the Same Direction*. In it, he comments on our insatiable need for quick-fix approaches to spiritual formation. Peterson observes that we crave answers in 30-second abridgments. It's impossible to prevent that from creeping into how we process the Christian life, especially during a transition.

The next two phases of a transition—the Evaluation Phase and the Alignment Phase—can often feel long and drawn out. They feel long because life processing takes time. Most of the time spent in a transition occurs during these phases.

A Christ-follower moves back and forth between evaluation and alignment. In the evaluation, God begins to reveal truth and refine the heart. As He reveals areas of sin or struggle, He calls us to repentance and surrender (1 John 1:9). Surrender and forgiveness bring new life and direction.

The quest for answers and a quick fix often comes from a self-induced pressure. It's inherited from today's Christian culture. Struggle and toil clash with the popular Christian "life gospel" of our day. Yet, God uses this struggle to build depth and character needed to face the challenges ahead.

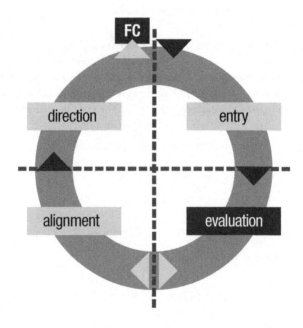

THE WATERLINE

Large ships impress me. They're most impressive when docked in port. At sea, off in the distance, they look small. But when we see them in port, up close, we realize how enormous they actually are.

When in port, these large ocean liners expose markings on their hull that can't be seen when plowing through the ocean. The waterline shows maintenance teams not only where the ocean's water comes up to on a daily basis, but also where most impact and corrosion occurs. Below this line is where the force and resistance of the ocean takes its toll, often unnoticed to most.

In the Evaluation Phase, God goes underneath to examine the damage and impact of the most recent voyage. This damage often goes unrecognized unless we're brought into port. Under the waterline, God begins to identify weaknesses and unseen cracks in a life.

Socrates famously said, "The unexamined life is not worth living." A life can be, and often is, transformed as one allows it to be examined. In the Evaluation Phase, God surfaces the actual values of a Christ-follower. The Christ-follower often comes face to face with his or her real self. These realizations can be disturbing.

In the Evaluation Phase, we discover that beliefs are not values. Values are life convictions born out of adversity and pain. When you're called on

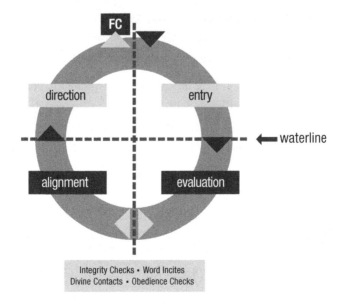

to fight for what you believe, you begin to stand for truth, as opposed to just being able to recite truth. During this phase, God begins to show the results of life lived without conviction, as well as purpose in the pain.

RESISTANCE

Most of us resist looking back. Too often, past evaluation appears either fruitless or too painful. We'd much rather avoid or skip this phase all together. But, inside each of us, our self-talk and evaluation rages on. We try to piece together why things have occurred, and what past struggles meant.

At some point, it's helpful to bring the conversation to the outside. It's also helpful to have questions to help frame the discussion. The key to finding answers is often being able to ask the right questions. Helpful evaluation can be organized around four categories of questions. These categories (from *Living a Life that Counts* by Tom Patterson) can help Christ-followers better process their past journeys and current circumstances:

- **What's right?** Where do you sense God's blessing? Where have you been affirmed? Where do you see God at work right now?

- **What's wrong?** Where are you experiencing your greatest struggle? Where do you need to focus greater efforts? Where are you in your journey with God? Where do find yourself resisting God?

- **What's confusing?** Where do you feel the most bewildered? Where are the pieces not coming together? Where does God want you to go, but you can't? Why not? Where is the greatest dissonance coming from?

- **What's missing?** Where is the greatest gap between problems and answers? Where do you feel free? Where do you feel most bound? Where do you need the greatest help? Where is your heart telling you that you should go?

PROCESSING TOOLS

It's also helpful to know that God uses four examination tools as He works under the waterline. These processing agents serve to refine a Christ-follower and help consolidate lessons during both the Evaluation Phase and the Alignment Phase. Knowing what God typically goes after during this time also helps an individual stay the course of examination and reexamination.

Tool #1: Obedience Checks

One of the primary ways God moves a follower through the time of evaluation and surrender is by creating moments to test our actual beliefs and behavior. These are called Obedience Checks. God often sends out the challenge to trust Him for the future and uses His Word to call for greater obedience. Obedience Checks build trust and dependency.

Obedience Checks present a crisis of belief. A Christ-follower is called upon to make decisions according to God's truth, as opposed to personal feelings. Either you believe that the Word of God is truth or you don't. Properly allocating time, setting priorities, relinquishing security, and moving beyond current comfort are all battles surrounding Obedience Checks.

Obedience Checks involve surrender—and, sometimes, re-surrender. Christ-followers often take possession of things, people, or entrustments that aren't theirs. Obedience Checks take followers to new levels of submission. Submission and following produce a greater sense of spiritual authority to a follower's influence on others.

Obedience Checks can also involve someone giving up a title or prestige in order to follow God's leading in another direction. Many followers get caught up in climbing the ladder of Christian organizations or the Church. Obedience Checks test issues of control and esteem.

Biblical Example: Abraham was willing to sacrifice Isaac, his only son. This brought him new power, clarity for the challenges ahead, and fresh dependence on God (Genesis 22:1-19).

Tool #2: Integrity Checks

God also uses transitions to test heart consistency. The purpose of an Integrity Check is to evaluate the consistency of inner convictions with outward behavior. Integrity Checks can come in the areas of money, resource allocation, priorities, use of time, sexual temptations, character challenges, relationships, or consistency of lifestyle. Integrity Checks seek to match words with deeds.

Integrity Checks often occur under the radar. In the quiet back alleys of our thoughts and motives, God begins to speak. As Christ-followers look back in their evaluations of the past, inconsistencies are revealed. Actions don't match espoused belief. A gulf grows between intended and actual behavior. Often, these private exchanges between God and a follower take place before they become evident to others.

God waits as a follower chooses to respond to His call for consistency. Followers may try to ignore these inconsistencies, but the battle within rages on. Integrity Checks reveal their need to go deeper with God.

Integrity Checks shaped the heart of David. Psalm 78:72 describes him as one who shepherded the Israelites with "integrity of heart" and "skillful hands." In a transition, God uses Integrity Checks to burn off false beliefs and refine convictions on which the future will be built.

Biblical Example: Daniel was challenged to compromise his commitments and convictions about God (Daniel 1:8-19).

Tool #3: Word Checks

Voice recognition is a core need during a transition. Transitions occur to build a greater capacity for recognizing and following God's voice. Christ-followers won't be able to recognize God's stirring and plans without a commitment to become mature in their use of God's Word. Christ-followers won't discover the deeper purposes of God in a five-minute devotional. Nor will they discover their unique contribution from a Sunday sermon alone.

Word Checks are about reengaging with God through His Word. In the Evaluation Phase, it's about using God's Word to help spiritually appraise the circumstances. In the Alignment Phase, it's about bringing behavior and plans under the authority of God's Word, regardless of feelings. Word Checks can lead to a paradigm shift on the part of a follower.

Word Checks are used by God to build discernment and wisdom, which can then be applied to life. Word Checks attempt to help Christ-followers discern whether the Word of God is truly a "lamp for my feet, a light on my path" (Psalm 119:105).

One of the main reasons Christ-followers derail during transitions is their loss of commitment to the Word of God. The Bible may have become an obligation or simply just another good book. Its Spirit-active power begins to lie dormant in a Christ-follower's life. The Evaluation Phase and the Alignment Phase are about creating a deeper hunger for guidance and direction. God will challenge a follower to return to His Word for answers and to act on their insights.

Biblical Example: Joshua was given a call from God to heed the word and truth that Moses had spoken to him—to not stray from the truth, but to let it guide his call to take the Israelites into the Promised Land (Joshua 1:1-10).

Tool #4: Divine Contacts

Divine Contacts are significant people, voices, relationships, authors, historical characters, or contemporaries who brush a follower's pathway just long enough to deposit critical truths or insights. They enter at critical moments and provide help, make resources accessible, provoke new insights, reveal new knowledge, and link a follower to new relationships.

Divine Contacts often come and go. Sometimes, however, they make a one-time appearance at a strategic moment in a Christ-follower's journey. They show up in critical moments for decision-making. They often provide key insights at just the right time. Visits from Divine Contacts are usually not planned; they are sovereign and divine providential occurrences.

Divine Contacts are used to affirm personhood and influence potential. They encourage and enhance development, while giving unique help or guidance. They can offer indirect advice or challenge a follower to greater intimacy with God. In the Evaluation Phase, Divine Contacts help reveal insights or assessment that a Christ-follower sorely needs. In the Alignment Phase, they can challenge a Christ-follower to surrender to and embrace the truth.

Biblical Example: Barnabas was a Divine Contact for Paul, sponsoring and helping Paul make the transition from what he was to the significant role he played in the future of the Church (Acts 11:22–26).

ABANDONMENT?

A new Christ-follower often consistently gets answers from God and feels the results of being chased and romanced by God. We sense His presence and its reassurance, and we build our lives on the promise that He will never leave us or forsake us (Deuteronomy 31:6).

At an undefined point, however, it sometimes appears that God begins to step back, almost as if to abandon the Christ-follower. His closeness seems to vanish.

It's not betrayal, but God beginning to build depth into our relationship with Him. He chased us, and He will continue His pursuit of us. But Christ-followers now begin to see our role also as pursuers of God. Like lovers in pursuit of each other, our pursuit of God now meets His ongoing pursuit of us.

Transitions often break the habits that can form from religion. The Christ-follower's life isn't about duty and responsibility—it's about relationship. It's not about us performing acts that please God, but a passionate love affair that transpires between us and our God and our trust in Him alone.

Transitions don't represent abandonment, but, instead, facilitate a deeper intimacy with Christ. Much of this new work is the result of work done under the waterline.

UN-STUCK: APPLYING IT

Most likely, the Evaluation Phase will produce moments of truth when a follower comes face-to-face with issues of self. Evaluation often produces an incredible need for God, as well as a re-encounter with the love and grace of God.

Consider the following:

- What has surfaced now as you think through the Evaluation Phase of a transition? What have you learned to value as a result?

- Look back at the four categories of questions on page 52. Apply them to your current transition and evaluate what led up to your transition.

- What makes you feel stuck? What is God going after?

- If you could address one issue right now, what would it be?

In this chapter, we talked about the back-and-forth time of a transition as God moves a follower from evaluation, alignment, and surrender to His new work.

In the next chapter, we'll talk more in depth about aligning to God's desires and purposes. Alignment and surrender is actually the defining moment of a transition.

7

alignment

The purpose of the Christian life is not to fill our heads with doctrine, but to awaken us to a spiritual quality of life that excites, energizes, and enriches us with a more genuine human life.

—JAMES HOLSTON, *THE TRANSFORMING POWER OF PRAYER*

Once you find where the trail is, you are faced with a sobering truth—in order to go on, you must let go of what brought you here. You cannot go on without turning your back on all of the very things that brought you to this place.

—MIKE YACONELLI

Some friends of ours had been living under the waterline for a long time. We questioned God with them. Their transition just seemed far too difficult and far too long.

Back and forth, back and forth, they responded to the evaluation work in their hearts with times of genuine surrender to God and His will. But, with regard to their future, the silence from God continued. Would their transition ever end?

They made repeated attempts to try to get their life direction back on track, only to experience another false start, another dashed dream. The husband even moved himself to Los Angeles and Hawaii in attempts to bring an end to all the uncertainty, only to find himself quickly back home again.

They were now cleaning out a rental unit and living on-site in the apartment provided. As their friends, we had concluded for God that enough was enough. It was easy to see why they became gun-shy, afraid to even think they could any longer hear God's voice.

One night, we met for dinner. Inevitably, they began rehearsing the circular story of options with little leading from God. They could do nothing else but pray.

It was obvious that they were still in the middle of their transition. As they shared their frustration, I gently mentioned that it appeared as if they were still in the Evaluation Phase and that no matter what they did, God would decide when the transition would end. My words were met with quietness. Everyone, including myself, wanted a better answer than that.

Those were hard words to say. It was very apparent that they had genuinely surrendered their future to Christ. Yet, the more they tried to figure it all out, the worse things got. Would the Lord make them surrender their home? Was it God's plan to disappoint their kids with the lack of funding for college?

Like Peter, they were left with the words that express the feelings of many who live in the midst of an ongoing transition: "Lord, to whom shall we go? You have the words of eternal life" (John 6:68). Their brokenness and struggle were part of the long obedience of a transition.

There's no formula for breaking out of a transition. But there's a promise. It's a truth modeled by Christ himself. In John 5, Jesus reveals an essential truth that came from his daily surrender to the will of the Father: "Very truly I tell you, the Son can do nothing by himself; he can only do what he sees his Father doing, because whatever the Father does the Son also does. For the Father loves the Son and shows him all he does" (John 5:19-20).

The prize of surrender is revelation. Every transition will consist of defining moments. It's here when a follower must once again affirm his or her allegiance to Christ and His purposes, whether answers come quickly or not at all. That surrender provides the seedbed for new direction.

In the Alignment Phase, the truth introduced in *Experiencing God* by Henry Blackaby rings true: every Christ-follower will reach a crisis of belief. This crisis of belief takes a follower back to that moment of giving control of one's life and one's future back to God. Transitions build dependency.

Issues of surrender can surface through a variety of means: personal wounding, insights from God's Word, small group accountability, confrontation from a friend or foe, a coaching call, or simply a time of quiet reflection. One thing is sure: realignment breeds the need for a decision.

God also uses alignment to go after the impediments and obstacles on the road ahead. Here are a few obstacles Christ-followers may confront as they contemplate moving forward during a transition:

- **Strong egos:** One way many of us protect ourselves from hurt or the unknown is through our sense of self-sufficiency. By running the show and calling the shots, we insulate ourselves from not being able to influence our future direction.

- **Shame or guilt:** Memories of past struggles and secret sin often still hold us captive. The depth of past pain holds us back in fear.

- **Lack of self-acceptance:** Many of us have not truly accepted God's grace and deep enduring love. We struggle to break free from past memories and move into new life.

- **High achievement:** Hard work and persistent efforts could have brought achievement and success. Turning off our high capacity for "doing" in order to experience a new world of "being" is a foreign idea —and one often rejected.

In the Alignment Phase, something is always given up in order to gain something better for the future. What it is differs for each follower. For me, it's been the approval of other people.

God's alignment call to me is often to exchange the approval I get from others for the approval I already have from God. I've often desired the acceptance from my peers more than God's presence in my life. I've been to that altar of confession many times. Each time I go, I join Christ in the laying down of my own agenda, the titles, the praise, and the temporal pats-on-the-back in exchange for living out my unique calling in the extension of God's kingdom. That moment of true surrender has brought personal renewal and directional clarity.

This alignment readies the Christ-follower for God's revealing of the future. Destiny experiences are moments where Christ begins to lift the fog and bring clarity to what lies ahead.

UN-STUCK: APPLYING IT

The prize of surrender is revelation. Most want revelation. Few want to surrender.

Look again at the four obstacles described above. Which one(s) could keep you from surrender? Don't get stuck in the Alignment Phase—your future depends on it. Lay down anything that may keep you stuck here.

In this chapter, we saw how God does a new and deeper work in a transition, often visiting our past wounding. The prize of surrendering (or aligning) to what God focuses us on yields new insight and revelation from God.

In the next chapter, we'll think through all that's involved in letting go of what once was, so that God is free to do a new work in the life of His follower.

8

letting go

Our first, most spontaneous response to pain and suffering is to avoid it, to keep it at arm's length; to avoid, circumvent or deny it...Befriending it seems at first masochistic. Still my own pain in life has taught me that the first step to healing is not to step away from pain, but to step toward it.

—HENRI NOUWEN, *LIFE OF THE BELOVED*

There is something of Jacob in all of us, I think. If so, there must be a night of reckoning for us, as well. A night when God finds us alone, grabs us, throws us to the ground, and wrestles with that fundamental flaw in our character. In the dark night of the soul, though he cripples us, in the dawn He blesses us. For some of us, the crippling is the blessing.

—KEN GIRE, *REFLECTIONS ON THE WORD*

One of the keys to a transition is to let go of the past in order to embrace the future. In a transition, a Christ-follower is often called to leave behind the familiar.

At this moment, God isn't in a hurry. We often are, but He isn't—especially during a transition. God is at work on a long-term project: shaping our hearts and life direction. It's not enough to agree or even resonate with concepts, especially if you're currently in a transition. Sometimes, it's important to wrestle with truth.

A transition is a sacred space. What follows in these next few pages is a time of guided spiritual reflection. Its goal is to help you process through your thoughts about transitions, or help you process your current transition.

Books like this often introduce new paradigms, provide information, and challenge the reader, but then just move on.

Structured time with God can bring freedom. Although you may want to move on in your reading, please take the time to do this exercise.

OVERVIEW

The following reflection exercise has been modeled from the *Benson Devotional* and a reflection journal created by Jim Branch. You can complete it in one sitting or over several days. The deeper you are into a transition, the longer you should take.

Start by using the Opening Prayer to focus your attention and heart. Next, spend time reading and praying through the Psalm. This is a practice from the early church. Don't just rush through. Instead, pray and reflect as you read. Next, read the Scripture Readings (together or one for each day).

Then, look back through the chapters we've covered so far in the book (chapters 1-8). Revisit the quotes at the beginning of each chapter. Reread the concepts that you underlined or that most impacted you. Go slowly, allowing time for reflection and listening.

Journal your thoughts. Write down what you find yourself thinking about. Finally, turn your thoughts into written prayers. Write and listen to God. Don't hurry past this necessary time with Him. Use the Closing Prayer to conclude the exercise.

Opening Prayer

Lord, I give it all back. Take and receive all that I am and have. You've given it to me; I give it all back to you. Do what you want with me. Just give me your love and your grace and that's enough. (Adapted from St. Ignatius)

Psalm 130 — Read, ponder, and pray your way through this psalm.

Scripture Readings

Colossians 3:1-17
Hebrews 12:1-13
Mark 8:31-38
Romans 12:1-2
Philippians 3:1-14
1 John 2:15-17
Genesis 22:1-19

Readings for Reflection

Review the quotes at the beginning of chapters 1-8. Spend time reflecting on the earlier chapters. Journal your thoughts and insights on the Transition Journal below. Think about how each passage relates to both your personal journey and your new understanding of entry into a transition.

Time for Listening

Spend quiet time with God just listening for His voice. Even if you find the discipline of silence difficult, practice being quiet before God.

Closing Prayer

Lord God, help me leave behind all the thoughts, actions, and attitudes that do not reflect Your delight and design for my life. May everything else pale in comparison to a new closeness with You. May You become my passion again. May You be my one delight. Amen.

UN-STUCK: APPLYING IT

Use the journal page below to complete the above exercises.

In this chapter, we've chosen to not race ahead, but, instead, provided the time and space to hear God's voice and sense His presence as result of aligning with His purposes.

In the next chapter, we'll move onto the Direction Phase of a transition. In this phase, God moves a follower from somewhere to somewhere else.

YOUR TRANSITION JOURNAL ENTRY

Take a moment to complete the exercises from the previous page.

9

living it forward

*We may ignore, but we can nowhere evade the presence of God.
The world is crowded with Him. He walks everywhere incognito.
And the incognito is not always hard to penetrate. The real labor is
to attend. In fact, to come awake. Still more, to remain awake.*

—C.S. LEWIS

*It was as though someone gave me permission to do what I most
wanted to do. I felt something deep inside me relax, and say "yes!"
There was no audible voice, nothing dramatic save the starry sky,
but some deep part of me knew what I was about.*

—TIMOTHY JONES, *AWAKE MY SOUL*

Tears began to streak down my face as I sat quietly in my living room chair. Our family and four other families had left our homes and our familiar surroundings of Southern California and moved to Melbourne, Australia. God called us to go there and minister to the hearts and lives of leaders and their churches. I had given our ministry to God, but I hadn't given Him the future of our ministry.

It wasn't an audible voice, but it was one that I could clearly hear. God speaks in ways that are often not audible. He speaks to the heart. As I watched the police beating of Rodney King ignite Los Angeles into race riots, I suddenly knew that God was speaking.

Terry, it's time to go home!

"But, Lord?"

No. Lay it down, Terry. I am ready to take you and the ministry in a new direction.

I had spent the past several months before that moment trapped in restlessness and self-evaluation. The ministry needed to be developed, but I'm a pioneer. I was stuck! My time of evaluation had many moments of surrender. I had given over the ministry, the staff, and even the decision as to who was to be the new leader. However, I had not given the future over to God's control. I had never envisioned that my work there might be finished. This was the moment of my final surrender. I had entered the direction phase of my transition.

Transitions do end. Not all endings mean a change in job or geography, but this time it meant both for me.

Breakthrough often comes at unexpected moments. It can come as the result of a chance conversation or a throwaway line, on the edges of a new thought, from reading a book, from attending a workshop on a completely different topic, from an extended time in Scripture, or during a TV newscast. God uses a variety of methods to break in on a life and bring new direction.

Moments like these are not the end of a transition, but typically represent the beginning of the end.

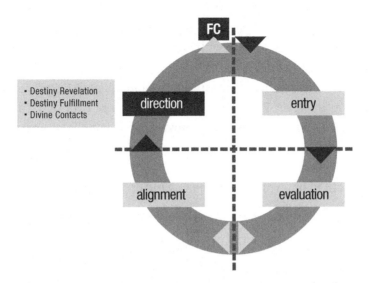

DESTINY EXPERIENCES

All Christ-followers experience destiny moments whether they recognize them or not. In these occurrences, God seeds the future. Destiny Processing refers to special experiences or events that contain insight into where God is preparing or leading a life. Christ-followers who finish well have a growing sense of destiny on their lives. As a transition begins to end, a series of destiny experiences will occur.

In destiny experiences, a Christ-follower senses that God is uniquely present. Such an experience can be a single awe-inspiring event or a series of events joined together. With destiny experiences, Christ-followers begin to sense that God is preparing to show them the way forward. These experiences aren't easily forgotten.

Scripture provides many examples of destiny experiences: Moses' experience at the burning bush (Exodus 3), Samuel's learning to recognize the voice of God as He spoke to him at night (1 Samuel 1-2), and Paul's dramatic encounter with Christ, as well as his blindness from the light (Acts 9). The biblical character who most embodies destiny experiences, however, is Joseph. He's a good example of how negative experiences could work together for good.

Joseph's brothers sold him into slavery. He was taken by a Midianite caravan to Egypt and sold to an important military leader. Eventually, during a discouraging experience in prison, Joseph was providentially put in touch with a palace official with whom he had favor because of his ability to interpret dreams.

Joseph's difficulties coincided with a crucial moment in Egypt's history. His ability to interpret Pharaoh's dream and his wise counsel facilitated Joseph's rise to a high position in the government. Joseph's ultimate contribution surfaced as a result of his destiny experience, preserving Israel during the impending famine.

God breaks in on lives in the same way today. Destiny experiences:

- Affirm God's presence, even in dark and discouraging moments
- Reveal insight into God's plan and how He uses Christ-followers
- Change others as they watch God move in the lives of His followers

We'll explore three types of destiny experiences: destiny revelation, destiny fulfillment, and divine contacts. But first, some real life.

REAL LIFE

Life planning is a two-day consultation that I do with Christ-followers. It's particularly helpful for those in transitions—those who need to sort out the past in order to better understand what God may want to do in their future. It usually involves my being in an intensive one-on-one experience with a person in transition. Recently, I spent two days not with just an individual, but with a couple. The husband was experiencing the transition, but they both needed to discover what might be next.

Richard had a pattern of God leading him through destiny experiences. When we shared the Transition Life Cycle (chapter 4), he was deeply affected. We determined that he was on the verge of moving into the Direction Phase. He had experienced an extended time of evaluation and surrender. Now it was just a matter of God's timing.

Our time together was the occasion for an unusual visitation from God. Richard and his wife discovered new clarity for their future. My consultation normally includes three coaching calls following our two days to ensure greater implementation of the life plans we've scripted. Also, we typically meet again 30 days after the initial consultation.

However, only five days after our initial meeting, Richard called me. He said he needed to meet with me. Anxious and persistent, he told me that I had to hear what had happened.

In the life plan we'd developed, it was clear that God wanted Richard to get more training. His wife Gabriela set up an appointment at Simpson College in Redding, California. Richard did not have a bachelor's degree. However, he found out that Simpson had a policy that 10 percent of applicants to their master's program would be accepted without a bachelor's degree.

On the spot, Richard had been accepted to study in a program that would take him deeper into God's truth. God had revealed Richard's destiny to him. At that moment, and with that experience, Richard moved beyond surrender to direction and the end of his transition.

DESTINY REVELATION

Destiny Revelation often occurs after a series of preliminary destiny experiences. Destiny Revelation is the "aha" moment when a Christ-follower knows that he or she has heard from God. Months, maybe years, of journey are galvanized into a future direction.

As a Christ-follower acknowledges God's initiating work, the future begins to unfold. All the answers aren't present, but answers do begin to come. Destiny Revelation begins to speak to some of the unanswered questions and specifics about jobs, career, decisions, opportunities, and new directions. These providential circumstances help us recognize how God has been at work all along.

God often uses Destiny Revelation to:

- Endorse a decision or commitment

- Affirm a paradigm shift that has unfolded

- Affirm a new course direction or opportunity

DESTINY FULFILLMENT

God was with Joseph. This is obvious as you examine Joseph's life. However, it's rarely so obvious in our lives. That's not because destiny moments aren't occurring today. Instead, it's because we don't have eyes to see these destiny snapshots. Here are two biblical passages that speak to this reality in Joseph's life:

> Now Joseph had been taken down to Egypt. Potiphar, an Egyptian who was one of Pharaoh's officials, the captain of the guard, bought him from the Ishmaelites who had taken him there. The Lord was with Joseph so that he prospered, and he lived in the house of his Egyptian master. When his master saw that the Lord was with him and that the Lord gave him success in everything he did, Joseph found favor in his eyes and became his attendant. (Genesis 39:1-4)

> Because the patriarchs were jealous of Joseph, they sold him as a slave into Egypt. But God was with him and rescued him from all his troubles. He gave Joseph wisdom and enabled him to gain the goodwill of Pharaoh king of Egypt. So Pharaoh made him ruler over Egypt and all his palace (Acts 7:9-10).

Destiny Fulfillment vindicates the work that God has been authoring all along. Destiny Fulfillment is the moment when Christ-followers actually begin to see God's plan unfold. And Destiny Fulfillment causes others to follow.

God uses Destiny Fulfillment to build courage. The only thing that can be more terrifying than not knowing what God is doing is knowing what God is doing. What was previously unclear now becomes clear, and the future now requires new faith. A pathway forward has emerged.

DIVINE CONTACTS

In chapter 6, we introduced the concept of Divine Contacts. They are significant people or relationships that brush by a follower's path just long enough to deposit critical truths or insights. Divine Contacts surface at key moments to provide help, make resources accessible, reveal new insights, and link a follower to new opportunities and new relationships.

In the Direction Phase, Divine Contacts help bring focus, clarity, and much-needed new paradigms. They also appear at decision-making moments to provide counsel and guidance. God often uses Divine Contacts to affirm new direction.

FAITH CHALLENGE

The completion of a transition brings with it a test of faith. Every step into the unknown requires faith—not faith in one's own abilities, but faith in the faithful character of God. In the end, every transition also brings on a challenge to one's ability to trust God.

Faith Challenges can occur in a variety of circumstances:

- Provision of financial resources

- Enacting of vision

- New job

- New ministry opportunity

- Relational trust

- New leadership challenges

- Family confrontation

- Emotional needs and concerns

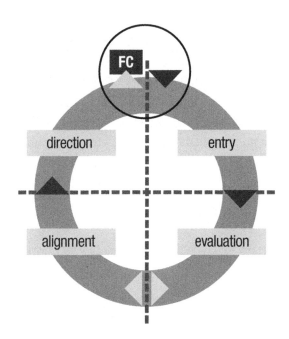

Esther's life message is that God can use an "ordinary person" to overcome impossible circumstances. But it takes faith. Mordecai challenged Esther by telling her she had attained royalty "for such a time as this" (Esther 4:14). God required Esther to risk her life and ask King Xerxes to spare the Jews. As a result of her Faith Challenge, the Jewish people were spared and God's purposes were advanced.

Now, it's your turn. The end of a transition will require you to put your weight down on your faith and step out into the future.

UN-STUCK: APPLYING IT

Have you heard God speak? That may feel like a daunting experience. Let's process what might be occurring:

- What does God seem to be saying? What is the breakthrough? List experiences when you sensed God speaking to you in new ways. How does what you're hearing line up with Scripture? Your past? Counsel from those who know you best?

- What now appears possible that didn't before? What faith will be required?

Remember: Don't force the end of your transition. The Direction Phase will come.

In this chapter, we saw how a series of destiny experiences began to point the way forward for a Christ-follower. The future brings with it new challenges to trust God and walk in faith.

The next chapter is called "The Catch." It begins the next section of *Stuck!* by introducing the three major transitions that all Christ-followers will face.

10

the catch

Like the woman at the well, sooner or later, perhaps in a quiet, reflective moment, we must all come to terms with the honest truth that we were looking for more than we found thus far.

—M. CRAIG BARNES, *SACRED THIRST*

Be still, my soul: thy God doth undertake. To guide the future, as He has the past. Thy hope, thy confidence let nothing shake; All now mysterious shall be bright at last. Be still, my soul: the waves and winds still know. His voice who rules them while He dwelt below.

—KATHARINA VON SCHLEGEL, *"BE STILL, MY SOUL" (HYMN)*

Some transitions are more strategic than others. There are three defining moments critical to the development of a Christ-follower. God often uses these three transitions in particular to interrupt the normalcy of life and shape lives in new ways to count for the extension of His Kingdom.

THE CATCH

The crowd automatically comes to a hush when they enter. The flyers climb the ladders to their small perches, high above the crowd. The announcer speaks of their heroic family heritage as they make their way to the top. All eyes, including mine, are now fixed on the small platforms. We're here to see the circus's most death-defying act: the high-flying trapeze artists. For me, this is the draw of a circus.

How would they do it? Why would they do it?

As I watch, I recall earlier years when safety nets were optional.

These are showmen, with smiles fixed in place. They slap their hands together, sending plumes of chalk up into the air.

The climb to the top was the first step to a performance that is now center stage. An empty swing is put into motion. It swings back and forth. The circus's most dangerous event is now ready to begin.

Off to the side, often unnoticed, another brave person climbs a solo rope. He is the catcher. He will take his position on a swing, also high above. At this point, little attention is given to him. He soon begins his rhythmic swing, matching the timing of the vacant bar, floating upside down. His size and strength are impressive. The flyers, though, are more dependent on his skill and strength. He will be important soon.

For just a moment, there seems to be some doubt as to whether the flyer will actually leave the security of the platform. Finally, he propels himself high into the air. He has broken free from the security of the perch and now progresses to the most important moment of the performance.

The speed of the swing, combined with his continuous climb in height, is a sheer thrill to watch. The flyer has now caused the first moments of the show to be long forgotten. Greater than the climb up the ladder—and the launch away from the platform—lies the most important moment of the show.

The catcher now comes back into focus. He has now marshaled a consistent pace in his swing: upside-down, back and forth. It now becomes apparent that the flyer seeks to match his rhythmic pace.

At the signal of the catcher, known only to the flyer, the time has come for the flyer to choose to do what seems unthinkable. To fly unattached from the security of the swing seems foolish. The danger is already great enough. What's planned is not only an unhindered leap into the air, but also a somersault—and one unique to this performer.

At the moment of truth, the sightline of the flyer becomes blurred. He must now rely on what has been practiced over and over again and the trust that exists between himself and the catcher.

The catch by the catcher produces applause reserved only for this unique moment. In the eyes of the catcher is now a securing smile. It is done.

The flyer is home. They have succeeded at what they have practiced and rehearsed. They have accomplished what few have ever dared to attempt. They have once again shown to everyone what they and few others are capable of doing. The repeat of the somersault back to the bar and then onto the platform serves only to reinforce an act of death-defying proportion. As the crowd files out, the dreams of the children have once again been fed. *One day*, they say to themselves, *one day I, too, will fly.*

This dramatic account of the trapeze act offers a vivid picture of three defining transitions in the life of a committed Christ-follower.

The first, the Awaking Transition, involves the decision to climb. It embodies the ascent to purpose. At some point, Christ-followers must step over a line and believe the truth that there is something more to life. They begin to believe that there is more to life than just our day-to-day existence. In fact, there's a God-embedded purpose in each life. But this purpose requires a pursuit.

The second, the Deciding Transition, involves the push and rush of propelling one's life of self-imposed boundaries out into an intentional life of meaning and service to the King. Life is now viewed differently—from God's perspective. The Christ-follower joins the grand narrative. Life lived differently now becomes the consuming passion of life. But it's not just about a contribution; it quickly evolves into a journey about intimacy. The knowledge of God and the pursuit of the holy now become an even greater passion than the pursuit of a task.

The third, the Finishing Transition, can only occur because of the first two. This transition involves a release from all that is familiar, as well as the convergent life that culminates in the knowledge that "for this I was born." It's about courage and trust. It's not about imitating the successful, but about being fully content with being the person God has known since before birth (Psalm 139).

In this final transition, being and doing come together as one. Being yields a doing that is godly in character and contribution. The ending is known by many as "union life." It involves bringing all of who you are to the few things God has called you to do.

Jesus is the catcher. He is the one who reaches out and catches us. He challenges us, pushes us, and shapes our lives and contributions to furthering His Kingdom. And He is the one who catches us by the hand.

Matthew 14:22-32 describes the story of Peter and his encounter with Jesus after stepping out of the boat and walking on water. When Peter began to sink, Jesus "immediately" caught him by the hand.

The chart below shows the three defining transitions in the lives of Christ-followers and the approximate ages at which they typically occur. Let's explore each of these transitions in greater depth.

THREE STRATEGIC TRANSITIONS

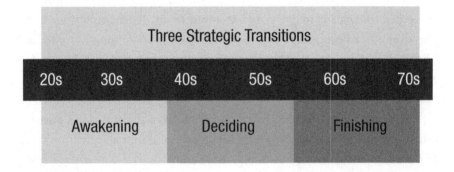

AWAKENING

Somewhere between the ages of 20 and the mid 30s, the first of the three major transitions often occurs. It is birthed out of a "holy" restlessness. There's an anxiousness to move in a significant life direction. The restlessness and discontentment create a new hunger for meaning and purpose. This transition is fueled by a deep resolve to do life differently—to not blindly follow what culture, peers, and others have defined as "the good life."

This first transition is focused on calling and clarifying one's life direction and values for the future. Common questions revolve around "should I?":

- How should I live?

- What's important?

- In which direction should I head?

- What course should I set?

- Is it possible to follow my heart and head out on a different path?

- Do I really have what it takes?

Because this transition occurs in one's early years, it's often mixed together with the challenges of establishing a career, becoming married, proving one's self-worth, and trying to define the criteria of success. Chapter 11 will explore this transition even further.

DECIDING

The second major transition often occurs between the early 40s and mid-50s. More than a mid-life crisis, it involves sorting through issues of priorities, meaning, and contribution.

As pressures begin to grow with career and family, bills and payments, and meeting the other costs of life, questions of priorities and decision-making come to the forefront. This transition often centers on deciding what one will not do in order to surface what one must do. The core issue here is this: how does one say "no" to the good in order to say "yes" to the best?

Questions that often accompany the many challenges of life and ministry during this period include:

- What are the few things I'm supposed to focus upon?

- Isn't life supposed to mean something more than just surviving?

- Is there any time for me and the passions of my heart?

- Could I really live according to my passion or calling?

- How do I decide? What's my grid for making the right choices?

The Deciding Transition is primarily about choices. It involves the quest to move beyond success and significance to uncover Kingdom contribution. Chapters 13 and 14 will explore this transition further.

FINISHING

This final of the three key transitions is about legacy and empowerment. It focuses on identifying one's ultimate contribution and it typically occurs in one's early 60s and beyond.

There's something to live for beyond the idea of retirement. This transition centers on understanding what God has entrusted to a Christ-follower and how to empower others to take those resources and multiply their impact. It's about living beyond one's days.

In the Finishing Transition, a Christ-follower's paradigm takes its final shift: away from position to influence through others. The focus is on relational empowerment—that is, with whom do I share that which God has entrusted to me? Convergence occurs when an individual ministers out of who they truly are. Chapters 15 and 16 will explore this transition.

UN-STUCK: APPLYING IT

The following six chapters examine in greater depth each of these three key transitions.

Go back and review which of the three transitions most closely approximates your current situation. What are the issues you're currently facing? What questions do you find yourself asking?

In this chapter, we introduced the three major transitions that occur in the lives of leaders and Christ-followers. These transitions keep them moving in their development as they seek to finish well.

The next chapter will go deeper into an explanation of the Awakening Transition, the one that clarifies the calling and life direction of a Christ-follower and leader.

11

awakening

The road to faith passes through obedience to the call of Jesus. Unless a definite step is demanded, the call vanishes into thin air.

—DIETRICH BONHOEFFER

The healthiest exercise of the mind of a Christian is to learn to apprehend the truth granted to it in vision. By prayer and determination we have to form the habit of keeping ourselves soaked in the vision God has given…The difficulty with the majority of us is that we will not seek to apprehend the vision; we get a glimpse of it and leave it alone…It is not a question of intellectual discernment or of knowing how to present the vision to others, but seeking to apprehend the vision so that it may apprehend us.

—J. OSWALD SANDERS

ALMOST REAL LIFE

The hour was late. The young entrepreneurs who had gathered here this evening were now vacating the cafe. They make sure to choose offbeat local places. Never do they meet at a chain coffeehouse—it's a matter of principle.

No one really plans the meetings. Everybody just shows up. No pressure. No agendas. They just know they want to be together. Being together is more important than doing life alone.

Tonight's gathering was different! They're usually not so serious. Tonight was almost combustible. Most walked away pumped. Some just walked away.

Seated at a hidden corner table, writing feverishly, is the writer of the group. She's scribbling at the pace of her racing heartbeat. Her tattered journal shudders from the speed at which she records her thoughts from the night.

She pauses as her fingers cramp.

Lord, you can hear the pounding in my heart. I'm tired of being on hold. I'm ready to move beyond. Before tonight, nothing I saw around me looked like who I know You are. And rarely do I see Christians passionate about their faith. But not tonight.

I've never been with people who think like me, feel like me, and want to live out their passion like I do, Lord.

Tonight, Lord, was more than just a coffee night.

Tonight was for me. You are moving me beyond despair and excuses.

Tonight, Lord, I heard the whisper of Your destiny for my life.

But, Lord, what's my next step? What direction do I take? And when?

School is done. I am done. Done working a job that means nothing!

Do I launch? Do I follow my dreams, or wait?

God, I need you now to be loud.

STIRRING

There is more to life. You can hear it in the passion of the young person writing above.

The Awakening Transition ushers in a quest—a quest for something more, for something different. The questions in this transition focus on what, when, and where. Many people know what they don't want, but often get stuck trying to answer the question, "What do I want?" This is common in the Awakening Transition.

Transitions often coincide with life stages. Finishing school, beginning one's career, marriage, starting a family, and more all affect the Awakening Transition. However, beyond life stages, something greater is occurring. The growing complexity of life brings to the surface deeper questions about God and life purpose, including:

- Who am I?

- What is it that I really want to go after?

- Why must I pretend that I'm fulfilled when I'm not?

- How can I do things that make a difference?

This stirring that occurs in the Awakening Transition doesn't go away easily. Persistent frustration, restlessness, and confusion are key contributors to launching this transition. Early dreams have already begun to be pushed to the back of the closet, tucked behind all the new demands of life. Life fills up with the things of daily existence. God sees all of this and initiates a transition.

It's here that uncertainty and early disillusionment can send the young off to make their fortune or make a name for themselves. What's most needed is someone to explain the reality of transitions, as well as to believe in the power of the young person's dreams.

Young leaders need sponsors. They need more than to just be told how much potential they have. Instead, they need the opportunity to be placed into real work, not just busy work. They need someone who believes in them to the point of giving them a real opportunity.

For some, it's easier to just escape. It becomes too tempting to retreat to the beach or couch in quiet resignation. It takes courage to lean into this new challenge. God will not let the struggle be answered by quick-fix solutions. The restlessness continues.

THE AWAKENING TRANSITION

In the Awakening Transition, God stirs into existence a Christ-follower's call. The chart below shows where this transition fits into a person's life stages.

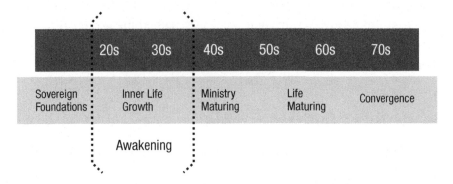

In the Awakening Transition, God purposes to do many things, including:

- Bring to the surface passion and early thoughts about potential life contribution
- Build commitment to living out one's personal calling
- Begin shaping inner character and influence
- Initiate discovery of one's sovereign shaping
- Help people identify like-minded laborers and bring to the surface potential options
- Launch a lifetime quest to follow Christ

The deeper questions of the Awakening Transition often fall into two categories. The first is self understanding: Who am I, really? How has God shaped me to make a difference? What makes me unique? The second is life direction: Where should I head? Should I take the chance and step out? If I were to get my chance, what would I do differently? What if I fail? Both of these types of questions point to the issue of personal calling.

CALLING

Calling is an individual's best-understanding-to-date of God's intention for his or her life. As God continues to work, the calling of a Christ follower unfolds. Calling is dynamic in nature.

The key to discovering one's calling for the future is to first gain perspective of how God has been at work in one's past. Perspective yields signposts that help inform where God might be leading in the future.

Whether because of a highly demanding career or because of a task-driven personality, some Christ-followers try to push past this early transition. It's common, especially for people in ministry, to not clarify their calling until their 40s. Whatever one's age, bringing clarity to call typically consists of four steps:

1. **Anchoring:** What has God taught you from His Word? This step entails reviewing your biblical calling and purpose as a believer. Biblical purpose anchors your personal calling.

2. **Assessing:** How has God shaped you in your past? In this step, it's important to understand your past development and life values as a believer.

3. **Discovering:** What is God calling you to accomplish? Discovering your personal vision provides direction for the future.

4. **Implementing:** How do you plan to accomplish your personal calling?

UN-STUCK: APPLYING IT

How would you answer if someone were to ask you about your personal calling? What would you say? What is the passion of your heart? If God could have His way in your life, what do you feel He might be calling you to be and do for His glory? Review the four steps of calling above. Which most addresses where you're currently in need of clarity or help?

In this chapter, we expanded our understanding of the Awakening Transition. Calling is the major theme of this transition that often occurs when Christ-followers are in their 20s and 30s.

The next chapter is different. It offers coaching questions and helps in the processing of the Awakening Transition.

MORE RESOURCES

Terry Walling and other invited authors have written a book on the Awakening Transition. *Awakening* goes deeper into understanding this transition and helps one to better understand God's shaping work. Learn more and purchase a copy today at www.leaderbreakthru.com/awakening

Leader Breakthru also offers those in the Awakening Transition an important personal discovery process called Focused Living. This personal development process (both as an online process or in a retreat format) walks you through the creation of a personal calling statement. Learn more at: www.leaderbreakthru.com/focused-living

12

questions

And now, Lord, with your help, I shall become myself.

—SØREN KIERKEGAARD

Transitions are about "voice recognition." As you travel through life, from here on, it's about voices...and which voice will you follow? Do you hear the voice of the One who made you, or the ones seeking to make you? Transitions help you value God's voice. It is the difference between just living and life. Life comes when you are better able to recognize His voice from theirs.

—TERRY WALLING

The glory of God is man fully alive.

—ST. IRENAEUS

When I teach about transitions in a class or training setting, there's often not enough time for all of the questions. Although we're confined to a book format here, I'd like to try to step outside its limits and recreate a conversation similar to those I've had with Christ-followers experiencing the Awakening Transition.

For the next few minutes, let's "grab coffee" and talk about the Awakening Transition. As you read, you might actually find yourself becoming drawn into the conversation. The conversation is generic, though your situation is unique. However, there are some common issues and traits that apply across the board. The Leader Breakthru website has much more on the Awakening Transition. To learn more, please visit www.leaderbreakthru.com/awakening

As we think about this first of three transitions, let me share some thoughts about what Christ-followers often feel and experience when they walk through this period.

First, you've entered something different in your growth and development. You aren't crazy; the restlessness you feel has a purpose. You're in a transition.

As hard—and maybe even as frustrating—as this time is, God is in it. He's at work. Something important is happening. God has moved in and has begun to proactively shape your life, your development, and your leadership.

God is calling you to something different in this life. You aren't just making up these feelings and rumblings going on inside of you. It's God. It's how He does things. God is in the business of shaping and molding lives. He uses defining moments like transitions to do a work that will carry you into the next phase of your development. He has done the same thing in all of us. An important process has begun in you.

Second, let me share some background. You may already know some of this. It's helpful, though, to hear again how God works in a life. God has always been at work in your life. There's never been a time when He hasn't been at work. Even through all these early years when you tested God and tried the patience of everyone around you, He was at work shaping your life. But now, His design is starting to emerge and become evident. He is confirming that there's a reason for your life beyond yourself.

As all of this now begins to emerge, you don't need to invest time in knowing who is at work stirring your heart. Whether it's primarily God or you is irrelevant at this point. What you need to work on now is determining "who" and "what" are driving you.

You don't have to wait to know whether God wants to use you right now. He can and He does. In fact, He's using you already. This incredible journey of finding your unique contribution in God's kingdom will unfold. But be ready! God not only wants you to know your purpose in life, but the value He places on you as a person. To Him, being is actually more important than doing. This Awakening Transition that you're now in is to help clarify your calling.

Does this make sense?

I say all of these things because your life and passions matter to God. This stirring in your heart is God bringing to the surface that which He has designed for you. He will from this point forward unfold a greater understanding of those plans. You and I struggle with the slowness of it all, but God's got time.

So, what has God brought to the surface so far? What are some of your core passions? What's the dream He's placed in your heart? You don't have to wait to know whether or not your life has purpose—it does.

So far, what vision or desire has He given you? In the next few months, new thoughts or thoughts from the past may begin to surface. Write them down. Find someone with whom to share them.

The key is to take hold of your future—but to do so loosely. Don't feel like you need to have all the answers. Just go with what you do know. Don't put yourself under the pressure of needing to have things all figured out, but allow yourself the freedom to explore. And as God brings new opportunities your way, try them and learn all you can.

I know you have other questions, but I want to make sure you know that I believe in this new work God is doing in your life. This is how I have seen Him work in others.

This transition will take some time. Don't get discouraged. Don't be surprised if it surfaces some struggles within you, as well as some inadequacies in others around you. Right now, the world is less than perfect. Try not to get cynical, but rather keep surrendering to God, asking Him to be your leader and to guide you through. Try not to fight Him. Instead, join Him.

As you work through all of this, I encourage you to consider some of the following helps:

- **Get a coach.** Someone who you can journey with. Not an "answer man," but someone with whom you can just check in on a regular basis.

- **Journal.** Get a notebook and keep track of ideas when they come. When new insights and dreams of the future rise to the surface, get excited! This is the God of the universe at work in your life. How cool is that?

- **Write out your personal calling.** This sounds harder than it really is. But it helps. What's is your best-understanding-to-date of who you are and what God wants you to do? Try to fit your statement on one page.

Be ready, friends. The enemy doesn't want you to clarify your calling. Well-intentioned people, including family and friends, can even get in the way of what God is at work doing. When this happens, give them some grace, but stay on course. It's important. You're important to God. Let me pray for you:

> *Lord, bless my new friend with Your favor and love. Communicate deep into his or her heart a sense of both Your approval and hope. Tell him or her that he or she is right where You want: tucked in next to Your side. Point the way now, Lord, and reveal the insights You have for him or her. Use this transition to solidify his or her commitment to You, and to reveal the first installment of the incredible journey ahead. I bless them, and Your work in his or her life in the days ahead. In Christ's name, Amen.*

REAL LIFE

He came into the world fast and premature. His birth occurred in just one hour. He hasn't stopped running since. There's no time to stop. There's too much to do and experience. He's passionate—always has been, always will be.

When he was small, his dad would sometimes grab him, pull him aside, get his full attention, and tell him to slow down. Now, the God who created him does that, and his father watches.

He spent his high school years wrapped up in sports and trying to be a friend others could count on. He's always been drawn to the real. He dislikes fake people, fake truth, and things that aren't done well. He gets that from his mom.

He doesn't care much about money. Instead, he's invested in relationships and family. All he's ever really needed was to know that someone would believe with him. He's now discovering that that someone is God.

It's become clear that he's now entered the Awakening Transition. He's fighting his current life circumstances. "What's the purpose?" is his challenge these days.

"I know that I'm supposed to do something, but I know it involves very little of what I'm currently doing," he says. "Why should I keep going through the motions?"

The evaluation period has begun. He knows he doesn't have all the pieces yet. Or even the big picture. He needs to go with what he has and see where it takes him. Simultaneously, God has opened up new opportunities. He's not without something to do, but inside he still has all the same questions. It's a challenge for him to just keep going. He has just a first glimpse of his destiny. At times, he's impatient for more.

One of my great privileges now, as his father, is to walk with him as God clarifies his calling. I'm praying for him to have both courage and patience. He and his new bride are gifted, and they're beginning to find their place and their role in God's Kingdom plan. Together, he and I are choosing to believe that the God who planted this great dream into his life will bring it into existence (Philippians 1:6).

The Awakening Transition sets the pace. It's directional in nature, affirming God's fingerprints and plan. This is the first hurdle of the steeplechase. Its purpose is to set into motion a series of events and life circumstances that unfold the sovereign backdrop to life: the revealing of one's personal calling and destiny.

UN-STUCK: APPLYING IT

What stands out to you about the awakening transition? Is this where you are?

What do you know about yourself? Are you impatient or a procrastinator? Are you most likely to run ahead or lag behind? How will who you are impact the processing of your transition? Who can help by traveling alongside you? Don't choose someone with all the answers, but someone committed to helping you process your questions.

In this unique chapter, we sought to provide coaching helps for those walking through the Awakening Transition, or for those coaching those walking through this first major transition.

The next chapter will examine the second major transition, the Deciding Transition. This transition helps Christ-followers develop a way to say "no" to good opportunities in order to say "yes" to opportunities that help to surface a follower's unique contribution.

13

deciding

Who am I really? What do you see in me that would move heaven and earth to capture my heart? My life feels like a collection of other people's expectations and disappointments. I do not know anymore who I truly am. Reveal to me my true identity, my place in your story. Give me grace to hear your voice; shut out all the other voices, and let me hear you alone.

—JOHN ELDREDGE

CLOSE TO REAL LIFE

His dinner at home grows cold. He spends many nights at the office catching up on emails and paperwork. As he works on into the night, he can't silence the voices from within: "Great company…Good staff…Great wife…Kids who love me…What's the problem?"

He's worked his whole life for this! There have been the adrenaline rushes that came from closing major deals. His name is above the building entrance. There is a sense of fulfillment. What he's built now provides for his family and offers jobs and benefits to the families of those who work for him. That is no small thing. But these alone aren't enough.

The endless frustration, the constant demands and repetitiveness of tasks, and his inability to give himself to things of core passion—all of these seem to move him further and further away from a true sense of meaning and purpose.

He's read the latest books, attended the top seminars, and hired coaches to help guide him through hard moments. But now there's a real sense of doubt that has eroded his belief. He questions whether life could be any different.

As he pushes paper, his self-talk breaks the silence of his office: "Where did all of this paperwork come from?…I thought this is what secretaries are for!…Are we having fun yet?…I'm sick and tired of my life!…All I do is paperwork every night!…Lord, what is it You want from me? You know I'll do it…I just want to be sure it is You talking to me…I'm so tired of all this…It's so much easier to just escape. More fun, too!…Maybe on the way home I'll pick up a six-pack and see if there's a game on."

A knock at his door jolts him from his monologue. It's Pete from sales. Startled, he invites the late-night intruder into his office.

"Hey, I thought I heard voices!" Pete starts. "I didn't know you were still here."

"Ah, yeah, Pete, what's up?" he replies.

"I was wondering if you had a couple moments to just talk about last quarter's sales projections," Pete says.

"Sure! Have a seat."

And so it goes on.

THE DECIDING TRANSITION

The second key transition is the Deciding Transition. This transition brings to the surface the need for intentional choices. But it isn't just about doing. Instead, it's also about the call to be. Effective life and ministry must flow out of being—that is, who you are.

There's a temptation in life to often just let things slide. Important questions remain important, but hide in the "not urgent" basket. In a transition, God raises the questions and then allows them to go unanswered to test how much we really want to know the answers.

Christ-followers are often surprised by what begins to pervade their thinking. What once seemed untenable now easily slips under the radar. Avoidance, and even denial, begins to make choices for us. Doubt and despair can also settle in. The Deciding Transition can come at a time when life makes some of its biggest demands on an individual. Job challenges, children and their schooling, marriage pressures, and church demands all sneak up on the weary. In the midst of a deluge of duties and responsibilities, questioning begins.

As with other transitions, the Deciding Transition passes through the four phases: Entry, Evaluation, Alignment, and Direction. Committed Christ-followers often begin to plateau in their passion and zeal for God and even lose their faith. In fact, some of the greatest amount of attrition from the Christian faith happens around this transition. To not decide is to decide. The result can be powerless believers facing the full-court press of the enemy's power.

The Deciding Transition is more than a mid-life crisis. And the answers aren't about working harder or smarter. Christ-followers must decide to follow Christ into the unknown. This transition is about moving off-road, onto a path less traveled.

In the face of this transition, some choose to medicate. Medication comes in many forms. Whether it's shopping, using the latest gadgets, seeking others' approval, dabbling in illicit relationships, over-eating, or any other form of self-gratification, committed followers are often just as susceptible to the lure of these short-term diversions. Sometimes, they're even more susceptible than the uncommitted. Why? Because they know the truth they're running from.

In the Deciding Transition, God begins to bring clarity to a Christ-follower's unique contribution. The chart on the following page illustrates when this transition occurs.

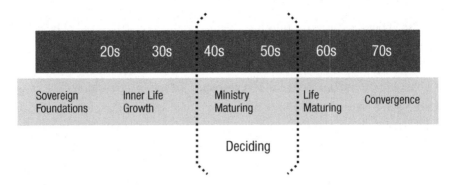

In this transition, God aims to accomplish the following:

- Bring to the surface uniqueness and contribution

- Heal past wounding and deepen intimacy

- Identify life messages and values

- Demonstrate a need for intentional spiritual formation

- Provide better decision-making grids for future opportunities

- Provide important first clues of ultimate contribution

The questioning that occurs during this transition often falls into two categories:

1. **Issues related to being:** Can I really hear God's voice leading me again? Or will all the other voices drown Him out? Can I follow Christ into a deeper healing and intimacy that I've only read about? Or will I fall back like so many others around me? Is the real Christian life even possible for me? Or will it just fade?

2. **Issues related to doing:** Can I really live my life out of my core passions? Or will life forever be what others want or need me to do? Can I come to terms with my unique contribution? Or will life just pile on more demands? Can I break free and do what I was made to do? Or am I stuck for life?

For many Christian business professionals, Bob Buford's *Halftime* brought to the surface the same issues that surround this transition. Buford tapped into this hunger that swirls around Christ-followers at this stage of their development:

I had not always paid attention to my life. To be honest, I only began paying close attention when I reached my early forties and found myself in a success panic. I was president and CEO of a tremendously successful cable television company. I was fully engaged in a good and growing marriage. We had a son who was—there is no other more appropriate way to say it—a prize…Yet there was something gnawing at me. How was it that I could be successful, so fortunate, and yet so frustratingly unfulfilled? (*Halftime* 12)

The second half of life is about deciding the best over the good. The first half was about exploring. The second half of life is about deciding and refining, especially in light of multiple options and responsibilities. Discovering one's role often brings breakthrough in the Deciding Transition.

What is it that you find yourself doing—whatever the environment—where you sense that God is using your life and that you are bringing honor and glory to Him? Whatever that is, it will help reveal your major role.

Role isn't about job or job descriptions. It's about the contribution an individual makes in each of the domains of life. Reduced to its essence, role is coming to terms with what you do as a follower of Christ. Role clarity often can provide a decision-making grid.

Role can be defined as the intersection of your natural abilities, your spiritual gifts, and your acquired skills. Of all the things you can do, what are the few things that you must do? You aren't defined by your job. There are better ways to describe what you do other than your title or position in life. Here are some examples:

- "I catalyze growth for others" vs. "I'm a teacher."

- "I help empower people to be who they already are" vs. "I work in human resources."

- "I care and nurture those who are most important in my life" vs. "I'm a stay-at-home parent."

- "I unlock potential in young lives and minds" vs. "I'm a coach."

The Deciding Transition brings clarity about role. Organizational demands can often silence an individual's core passions and calling. Who we are often gets lost in what others need us to do. Without the Deciding Transition, those questions might be lost forever.

REAL LIFE

The students who attend my doctor of ministry (DMin) classes sign up for them without really knowing what they're about. They have an interest in the topic of leadership development, but most who register are fulfilling a degree requirement. I'd estimate that over 80 percent of the students in my classes are in some type of transition.

Bryan was no different. He's an associate pastor working with young adults. "People said, 'Walling's class was good,' so I signed up" was how he introduced himself. He was looking for a class that would help him improve his leadership skills and finish his program.

The real problem, however, was that he was starting to plateau in his growth. By the second day, it was apparent that he was struggling to know which way was forward. He was facing the Deciding Transition.

Bryan gave no indication to others that he was anything but a cutting-edge, crisp-thinking leader. Yet, deep inside, he was spinning. He deflected and laughed off penetrating comments. When the direct hits headed his way, he dodged them. But his desperation only grew. He was struggling to know how to decide which way was forward.

Bryan's plate was full with a wide variety of tasks at his church, very few of which tapped into his core passions. The resignation of the senior pastor left him with more questions. This had pushed buttons that he'd been avoiding for years. He was acting out old patterns. All of this had kicked him into the transition. What was next?

The class discussion on transitions helped him to realize that he was moving from the Entry Phase to the Evaluation Phase of his transition. The class couldn't offer him all the help he needed, so he called me and we agreed to a coaching relationship. Soon, Bryan sat in my home for two days of heart searching, healing, and resolution.

Bryan was confronted with deciding what to say "no" to in order to say "yes" to what God has shaped him to be and to do. He decided. How about you?

UN-STUCK: APPLYING IT

What's important to you right now?

How would you define the contribution you make in the lives of others?

First, focus on issues related to being. Journal on some of the questions that have been bugging you lately. Next, focus on issues related to doing. Role reflects the intersection of spiritual gifts, natural abilities, and acquired skills. Examine each of those in your life individually. What do they look like in your life when they intersect with each other and work together?

In this chapter, we saw how followers begin to clarify who they are, as well as how to make intentional choices to move toward one's contribution.

In the next chapter, we'll go deeper into the Deciding Transition with coaching questions and processing helps.

MORE RESOURCES

Terry Walling and other invited authors have written a book on the Deciding Transition. *Deciding* goes deeper into understanding this transition, along with helping better understand God's shaping work. Learn more and purchase a copy today at www.leaderbreakthru.com/deciding.

Leader Breakthru also offers those in the Deciding Transition an important personal discovery process called APEX. This personal development process (both as an online process or in a retreat format) walks you through the creation of a personal life mandate. Learn more at: www.leaderbreakthru.com/apex

14

decisions

It was as though someone gave me permission to do what I most wanted to do. I felt something deep inside me relax and say "yes!" There was no audible voice, nothing dramatic save the starry sky, but some deep part of me knew what I was to be about.

—TIMOTHY JONES, *AWAKE MY SOUL*

Help me, O God, to listen to what it is that makes my heart glad, and to follow where it leads. May joy, not guilt, your voice, not others, your will, not my willfulness, be the guide that leads to my true vocation.

—KEN GIRE, *WINDOWS OF THE SOUL*

Let's "grab coffee" again. This time, we'll talk about the Deciding Transition. I hope you'll be drawn into the conversation and discover some insights that apply to you.

A TIME FOR DECIDING

Many Christ-followers aren't very anxious to talk about the Deciding Transition. Because of this, I've had discussions with many people that have led nowhere.

Many who face this time in their lives already know the choices God wants them to make. However, these are buried underneath stacks of life's demands. Often, they begin to doubt what God has placed inside of them.

Let me open with a few thoughts. First, all the things you're feeling right now—the struggles, obstacles, and lack of energy, even the feeling of being beaten down and ready to give up—all tell me you're in a transition. You're living in the in-between. And you aren't alone. Many have encountered these very same feelings. You're facing one of the most strategic crossroads in your journey with Christ.

Second, even though it may not feel like it, God's desire is that you experience a new level of clarity and focus and the ability to say "no" to some things so you can say "yes" to the right things. That's what the Deciding Transition is all about.

Let me see if I can help give you some perspective on this time of transition. God has always been at work in you. There's never been a time when He hasn't been at work in your life. The issue, then, is not whether God is at work, but rather what He is at work doing.

God matures followers through a series of phases in their development. You're just at the end of one important phase of your development and this transition is positioning you for the next. What makes this transition different is that a major shift is occurring.

You're experiencing what I call the Deciding Transition. You can only live out of duty and responsibility for so long. Now, God wants you to re-encounter His vision for your life.

This requires some sorting out because of what begins to happen in our lives. Things begin blocking our ability to hear from God: past struggles, hurts and wounds (some self-inflicted, some inflicted by others), and the demands of our jobs and other responsibilities that we carry. Some of these need to be sorted out. Some need greater healing.

God is using much of this to drive you deeper into Him in order to give you greater clarity to your unique contribution in life. You simply will not finish well in your life without this time to re-think what's important. From now on, your life will only make sense if you begin to move toward the few things that He wants you to do and to live from your interior journey with God.

Don't be surprised if God brings to the surface things from your past to teach you. These lessons are there to guide your journey forward.

Here are some specific suggestions to help you. Develop a timeline that helps you look at your journey thus far and identify some of the key turning points in your life. See if you can meet with someone to help you process what has occurred throughout your life. You're looking for the things God has deposited into your life. Some of these have come from your victories, while some have come through your pain.

Each of these turning points begins to point us to a role and contribution God has prepared for us to make in others' lives. Oddly enough, some of our greatest hurts or failures can be some of our most important turning points. Processing the pain of the past has real purpose: it brings healing to you, as well as help to others (2 Corinthians 1:4-5).

Next, consider this: of all that you've done, when did you feel God used you the most? What is it that you were doing or contributing? What do you bring to the situation?

See if you can identify the contribution you make. How does that same contribution apply to the role you play at work? At home? At your church? In the community? Ask others how God uses you to make an impact.

My guess is that you'll need some help in bringing greater definition to who you are and what you do. Who can coach you? Who can help you hear from God? This might be a good time to look for a spiritual director or guide.

Here are some final thoughts. All transitions take some time. There's a sorting out that must occur. You'll need to invest yourself in this task. Be aware that it will be much easier to hide, deny, or medicate yourself.

Heed this warning: many fall from the faith at this stage. Be careful! Protect yourself. Be intentional. Set up accountability. Commit to honesty.

You probably feel that you don't have time for all of this. You may be a person who likes action and getting things done. Even if you feel as if you don't have time to work through this transition, it's crucial for you to make time for it.

You're worth it. God will bless your efforts in your contribution and even in your legacy.

UN-STUCK: APPLYING IT

The Awakening Transition brings your calling to the surface. The Deciding Transition addresses your role and contribution to others. What do you need to say "no" to in order to move forward with God?

Review the dialogue in this chapter:

- Which part of the coaching resonated with you?

- What would you say is your contribution to others, or to the needs of a group? (At work, at home, at church or in your community, etc.)

- What need are you most passionate to address? What cause do you feel called to get involved with? What is the one thing you would love to do if we would allow you to do it?

(Note: The Leader Breakthru website has much more on the Deciding Transition. I encourage you to go there to find extended help: www.leaderbreakthru.com/deciding)

In this chapter, we offered helps for those processing the issues related to the Deciding Transition, and the resurfacing of being.

In the next chapter, we'll highlight and explore the third and final of the three major transitions, the Finishing Transition. This transition marks the decision required to finish well as a leader and Christ-follower.

15

finishing

The thing is to understand myself, to see what God really wants me to do; the thing is to find the truth which is true for me, to find the idea for which I can live and die.

—SØREN KIERKEGAARD

But it is important that in this world there remain a few voices crying out that if there is anything to boast of, we should boast in our weakness. Our fulfillment is in offering emptiness, our usefulness in becoming useless, our power in becoming powerless.

—HENRI NOUWEN, *REACHING OUT*

THE CALL TO FINISH

I was inside my house when I heard a loud crash. I ran outside and my friend Ron had fallen off our roof. He was gasping for air. The pain that engulfed his body could only be expressed in deep moans and sighs. We helped stabilize him, but his pain persisted. This wasn't what he had planned. Ron is a "doer." He was deeply involved in ministry, along with helping to rebuild our coffee-house church and being trained to lead a men's ministry. He was really beginning to find his stride and speak into men's lives. Why had he struggled for years to get to this point in his journey only to fall off our roof? It didn't make sense.

Ten broken ribs and two trips in and out of the VA hospital later, he was sidelined in a chair and as mad as he could be. God had stopped him in his tracks. Sometimes, God has to do that to get our attention. It's not all that un-common in a transition. Before He moves in, He allows us to recognize our need for Him.

Months before, Ron and I had discussed that he was moving into a time of convergent ministry. Convergence is the time when all of who a Christ-follower is meets what God has assigned him or her to do. It's when a Christ-follower realizes "for this I was born." Ron was close to that point.

After his fall, as we sat together, reflecting on his injuries and where he now was, I challenged Ron to use this time to go deeper with God and not fight Him. He wasn't ready to hear those words. A week or so later, we revisit-ed that conversation.

"Dang, I did not want to hear that, but you were right," he said. "All I'm do-ing is sitting in a chair and fighting God. He's got me right where he wants me!"

Ron was in the Finishing Transition. He's in his early 60s. His fall was part of the Entry Phase into that transition, and his pain began to subside, only to reveal that he had gone under the waterline. It was now a time of evaluation and surrender. The Finishing Transition is about final resolve and choosing what kind of end game you'll live. So much of what is next is tied to maintain-ing a deep, intimate relationship with Christ. The fall was Ron's call to go deeper in Him.

Some of the most profound questions are addressed during the Finishing Transition. These questions include, "Will my life have made a difference?" and "Am I committed to passionately serve Christ to the end?" These choices and the commitment to finish well set up this third transition. The challenge moves beyond success or accomplishment to passing on to others what one has learned. The Finishing Transition ushers in a time of legacy—that is, living a life that others will want to live and model (2 Timothy 2:2).

FINISHING

As Christ-followers grow older, they face increasing limits in their energy, resources, and capacity. But their influence can grow.

This transition often surfaces before one is ready. Sometimes, it's brought on because of transitions in organizations or career changes. Other times, a Finishing Transition launches because of physical limits or because of the cultural mandates of retirement.

Some Christ-followers become passive, resigned to what they see as the limits life presents. But for those who are ready, there is a new joy of allowing others to blaze the path. Their role has changed to travel alongside others. More than the idea of a sage mentor, this stage can be about passing one's legacy to others. The chart below helps identify the place of the Finishing Transition in a person's life.

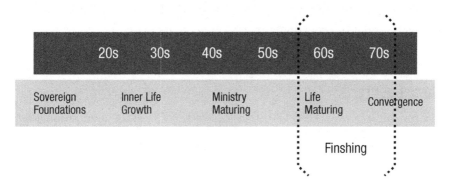

In this transition, God often purposes to:

- Inspire and challenge a follower with the notion of finishing well

- Move a follower into a convergence of being and doing

- Solidify a follower's clarity with regard to ultimate contribution and legacy

- Bring together lessons and experiences of past wounds and successes

- Dispense an increased spiritual authority to serve others

- Identify protégés who can be entrusted with one's insights and learning

Christ-followers often find themselves seeking answers to a series of questions, all framed around how one should view the finish. These questions include:

- Will my life have meant anything for Christ?
- Will my life have meant anything for others?
- Will my life have meant anything for the world in which I live?
- Will my life mean anything when I'm gone?

These lead to some other, important questions followers should be asking in the finishing transition, such as:

- Will I push to the end, bringing all of myself to what I do? Or will I simply retire, sit back, and let others do the work?
- Will I find my niche, keep learning, and stay in the game? Or will I let church culture push me aside in favor of the younger?
- Will I intentionally leave my legacy deposited in the lives of others? Or will I doubt my contribution and simply hope that others have appreciated my life?

RETIREMENT?

In his study of over 5,000 Christian leaders and Christ-followers throughout history, Dr. J. Robert Clinton discovered a startling truth: few leaders actually finish well. In fact, only about one in three do. Is it really acceptable that this is how the lives of Christian leaders and Christ-followers are supposed to end? Or is there more?

Retirement is a cultural phenomenon, not a biblical mandate. The end should be one's greatest contribution. Yet, many older Christ-followers retire to lives of self-indulgent leisure and, in turn, allow the younger generations to do the work. Others fail to groom mentors and pass them the baton.

Two extremes are modeled for us today. The first sounds like, "I've done my bit for the church. Now it's somebody else's turn," while the second sounds like, "These young people aren't ready yet, or else I'd turn over the reigns."

Both of these attitudes cause damage. The first comes out of a lack of developmental understanding of discipleship, the second out of a pathology of control and inflated self-importance.

Later years are to be guiding years. They aren't meant to be years of indulgence. The problem with self-indulgence is that you'll never have enough. Why should your life priorities change just because your career has?

The apostle Paul talked a lot about finishing. Here are a few examples:

- "Not that I have already obtained all this, or have already arrived at my goal, but I press on to take hold of that for which Christ Jesus took hold of me" (Philippians 3:12).

- "For I am already being poured out like a drink offering, and the time for my departure is near. I have fought the good fight, I have finished the race, I have kept the faith. Now there is in store for me the crown of righteousness, which the Lord, the righteous Judge, will award to me on that day—and not only to me, but also to all who have longed for his appearing" (2 Timothy 4:6-8).

The last years of life are also supposed to be lasting years. The wisdom, insights, and experience that come with age are to be honored and entrusted to those rising to new levels of influence.

Christians have made at least two major errors regarding aging. First, the western church has embraced our culture's worship of youth. In many areas, youth has become a requirement for success. Older people have been marginalized. Second, individual Christ-followers have fallen prey to living with a sense of entitlement—rather than servanthood—in the end.

"Retirement years" are not a reward. Instead, they are meant to be years of final contribution. The freedom that can come in later years should be devoted to service and fruitfulness. God has entrusted His followers with many life experiences over the course of their journeys and these should now be stewarded for others.

One's influence is not primarily the result of one's position. Leadership—not position—is primarily tied to influence. Whoever has influence has leadership. And influence is about relationship.

Older Christ-followers can still have influence if they can make this shift in their paradigms. The most important thing is not the position that they hold, but the relationships they're willing to forge. If older people are willing to enter into the world of younger people, they will be able to build relationships of influence. It's about depositing life lessons into a few, not many.

Finishing, though, is primarily about maintaining a vibrant love for and commitment to Christ. One of the greatest encouragements to younger leaders is seeing older Christ-followers still passionate about Christ and His call on their lives. One doesn't have to lead from the front to have influence. Influence is now about modeling a posture of lifelong learning and doing a few things well.

REAL LIFE

I wanted a mentor. But what I got was more than I'd bargained for.

I was feeling lost in Australia. I had taken my young family thousands of miles away from all that was familiar and was now drowning in the challenges of ministry and the limited time of our visitor visas.

I was mentoring leaders who had given me their trust to help sort through their development and leadership. But I needed a framework to ensure that I would truly offer real help. One day, I faxed Dr. J. Robert Clinton, who was teaching at Fuller Theological Seminary at the time, asking for help.

I was convinced that he would be too busy with his many responsibilities to help me personally, so I hoped he would recall me well enough to find someone else who could help me. To my surprise, Dr. Clinton replied that he was up for the challenge.

Weeks later, a fax arrived. It contained 14 pages of assignments. Dr. Clinton is a teacher. When you ask a teacher to mentor you, you get assignments. I didn't know at the time that this was his way of screening those he would mentor: if they were faithful enough to respond, then they were truly in a learning posture.

Fortunately, I did respond. Dr. Clinton (Bobby) has helped guide my development and decision-making ever since. His assignments and advice have been essential to my development. But an even greater influence on me has been how Bobby has lived his finishing years. His life at this stage of development and his empowerment of people like me have left a deep impression on myself and hundreds of others.

Bobby has modeled the life he teaches. He has sponsored a diverse group of leaders into ministry, embraced new technology, made changes in his teaching methods, cared for his physical health, moved closer to his family and their lives, and carefully chosen assignments and opportunities that help leave behind his legacy of ideation. The list goes on and on.

I've marveled as I've watched him say "no" to some of the things he can do well (influencing and teaching leaders) and "yes" to what he must do (finish his research in leadership development, write and mentor the few, etc.).

Bobby is finishing well. His example has inspired many to do the same. This may be the greatest impact of his life. His research has uncovered choices that can help other leaders finish well, too. These choices include repeated times of renewal, maintaining a posture of lifelong learning (along with critical habits of gaining a lifetime perspective), allowing personal calling and mission to be dynamic, and making a commitment to mentor and to be mentored.

To see someone embody a life message is to witness firsthand someone more in love with Jesus at the end than at the beginning. Bobby demonstrates that it's possible, even in our day, to be more passionate for Christ, more committed to the Word of God, and more willing to serve Christ even at the end of one's life. Bobby is having his greatest influence at the end.

CHOICES

The Awakening Transition sets the pace. The Deciding Transition gives clarity. The Finishing Transition directs a Christ-follower to his or her ultimate contribution and a passion to finish well. Why is it so important to talk about this before one gets there? Because today decides tomorrow.

UN-STUCK: APPLYING IT

What if you feel shut out by doors closed to you because of your age? Here are some ideas:

- Make sure that your paradigm is that leadership—not position—is influence. This is key to reopening doors.

- Adopt a few people. Identify a handful of Christ-followers who you feel God is working through and look for ways to insert yourself into their world. You should approach them, as opposed to waiting for them to come to you.

- Offer relationship, not advice. Time for advice from your past needs will come as a by-product of your ability to listen to their dreams for the future. Look for those who want to build a relationship and then invest yourself.

In this chapter, we explored the third major transition, the Finishing Transition. Retirement needs to be replaced with a focus on finishing well and leaving behind a godly legacy.

In the next chapter, we'll work through coaching helps in the processing of the Finishing Transition.

MORE RESOURCES

Terry Walling and other invited authors have written a book on the Finishing Transition. *Finishing* goes deeper into understanding this transition, along with helping better understand God's shaping work. Learn more and purchase a copy today at www.leaderbreakthru.com/finishing

Leader Breakthru also offers those in the Finishing Transition an important personal discovery process called Resonance. This personal development process (both as an online process or in a retreat format) walks you through the creation of a personal life mandate. Learn more at: www.leaderbreakthru.com/resonance

16

legacy

Let us labor for an inward stillness, An inward stillness and an inward healing, That perfect silence where the lips and heart are still, And we no longer entertain our own imperfect thoughts and vain opinions. But God above speaks in us, And we wait in singleness of heart, That we may know His will, And in the silence of our spirit, That he may do His will, And do that only.

—HENRY WADSWORTH LONGFELLOW

Are you in the midst of the Finishing Transition? Let the following thoughts filter through your life experiences—where you find yourself right now. At stake is the deposit of your life experiences into others who (1) may or may not know that they need what you have and (2) probably don't know how to access your help.

Let's head to our favorite "coffee shop" and talk one last time.

THINKING ABOUT LEGACY

As we think about this final of three transitions, let me start the conversation. As I "talk," try to listen to your heart.

I'm glad you're here. Just the fact that we're having this conversation is huge. You and I both know others who have fallen aside. Has anyone blessed you lately? I bless God and I thank him for you.

You're in the final of three transitions, the Finishing Transition. You don't need me to lecture you, but there are a few things that might help as you tell me your story and what you feel God has entrusted you to give to others.

We've got a problem in the Church. We worship the young and don't know what to do with the old. It's totally backwards from what we see in Scripture, yet we persist in our behavior. I'm sorry. Because of it, many like you are hurt and feel discarded. We need to go into this next phase of your influence for Christ with eyes wide open to that reality.

But there's a change that might need to occur within you. Up until now, you may have equated influence with position. You shouldn't see those as connected. Many may see it that way, but, in actuality, influence is relational. We both know that you have the potential to make a big contribution, so I want to encourage you to come alongside those in whom you see potential and pour your life into them from up front.

I'll stop now, drink my coffee, and give you a chance to process those thoughts. Reflect for me on what you already know about what God wants you to give away to others. Here are some questions that might help:

- Do you know what you know?

- Do you know what you do?

- Do you know what you have to give to others?

- When does God seem to really show up when you're just being yourself?

- What does God want you to focus on from here to the end?

- What's the best setting for you in which to live out that role?

- What do you think would please God the most? Would that tap into your passions?

- To whom do you want to entrust what you know?

- What few could most benefit from your lifelong learning and skills?

- How can you get near them to build relationships?

These questions are worth your time and reflection. I'd like to also offer some final thoughts, out of respect for your journey with God.

Don't stop. Don't coast. Don't just retire. This isn't the time to sit and let others do the work. The resting will come later. God has deposited things in your life that we, the Body of Christ, desperately need.

Don't let a job description or contemporary Christian culture dictate what you do. Be yourself. Show us how much you love Christ! Model for all of us, especially younger Christ-followers, what it's like to be more in love with Jesus at the end than at the beginning.

Run this final leg of the race. Ahead is the prize.

UN-STUCK: APPLYING IT

What causes a Christ-follower to finish well? What intentional choices can you make that will foster a life more passionate about Christ and His call at the end than at the beginning? Here are five choices. How are you doing?

1. **Mentoring:** Make the choice to allow others to speak into your life and shape it.

2. **Spiritual Renewal:** Make the choice to seek God repeatedly and with passion.

3. **Lifelong Learning:** Make the choice of self-care and becoming a lifelong learner.

4. **Perspective:** Make the choice to live and reorient your direction based on a sovereign perspective.

5. **Calling:** Make the choice to allow God's will and call to be dynamic and unfolding.

In this chapter, we offered coaching helps for those facing the Finishing Transition and those coaching those facing the Finishing Transition.

In the next chapter, we'll move to the final section of *Stuck!* In doing so, we'll explore together some ways to get all that you can out of a transition.

MORE RESOURCES

Take the Coaching Needs Assessment survey offered through Leader Breakthru and determine your areas of needed personal development and on-line coaching modules that will help resource your growth: www.leaderbreakthru.com/coaching-needs.

17

response

If you will acknowledge, recognize and pray—if you will commit yourself to this process of listening—you will begin to realize that the voice you have heard so often across the days of your life has been His voice.

—BOB BENSON, *HE SPEAKS SOFTLY*

The greatest saints are not those who need less grace, but those who consume the most grace, who indeed are most in need of grace—those who are saturated by grace in every dimension of their being. Grace to them is like breath.

—DALLAS WILLARD, *RENOVATION OF THE HEART*

City Slickers is a movie that depicts three frustrated suburban yuppies. They didn't want to just let life pass them by without at least making one attempt to bust free—in their case, this mean by "working" as cowboys on a cattle drive. Billy Crystal's character is the movie's philosopher. He's constantly trying to reconcile real life with the contrived experience of participating in a cattle drive.

The pivotal moment comes when the trail boss, played by Jack Palance, tells Billy, "All of life can be boiled down to one thing." The problem is that he doesn't tell him what that one thing is. Scene after scene, Crystal attempts to discover what he meant by "that one thing."

At the end of the movie, the characters determine that the one thing is about not holding back, not shying away from really living life—that resolving to truly live life could be one of life's most important lessons.

GETTING THE MOST OUT OF EVERY TRANSITION

There's one truth about transitions that needs to be embraced: Christ-followers ought to get everything that God has for them out of each transition He brings their way.

Don't waste your transitions. Use them to the fullest! Don't give in to the temptation to seek a quick remedy. This guiding principle can be fleshed out in three ways.

First, closely examine the events and experiences that have led up to each transition. Where were you before coming in? Explore various possibilities and paradigms that God might be introducing to your life.

Second, focus on deepening your intimacy with God and gaining a new understanding of His character. Live with greater dependency on God in your journey with Him. Recognizing God's voice in greater ways is one key purpose of every transition.

Third, and finally, look for patterns to how God works in your life, especially during past transitions. Move from there to attempting to discern the future according to how He's worked in the past. Make crucial choices that will align your life with the ongoing work of God.

Again, get all you can out of your transition. Fight the desire to bring premature close. Don't get discouraged with the length of your transition by thinking it'll never end. It will end. And when it does, you'll be left with the insights you had the courage to seek and wait for.

What happens when a follower realizes that things aren't working out despite his or her best efforts? Why isn't it better to just cut the losses and move on with a commitment to do things differently next time? Because opting out is to bypass what God's shaping work can do. A follower who bails out of a transition early will almost assuredly be forced to face and deal with these same issues again. Before making major life or ministry decisions, processing a transition first is always a better option than to leave prematurely.

Followers often need additional reasons for tackling each transition as it comes and not skipping it or bailing out early. The remainder of this chapter will explore reasons why Christ-followers can fail to stay the course and get all they can out of a transition.

BUSYNESS

In our world today, the lack of time is now the great crippler, whether one is a Christ-follower or not. The critical commodity of our culture has moved from money to time. Incredible demands are now placed on so few hours in a day.

People rarely argue about the importance of processing a transition. But the discussion quickly moves to the topic of time, or the lack of it: "When would I have time to do these things, Terry? How could I actually find time to read, study the Word for my own personal growth, take personal retreats, or get spiritual direction?"

These questions reveal how far off we are today. The tyranny of the urgent is now clearly in the driver's seat of our lives. No wonder we live in a post-Christian culture and society. No wonder the western church struggles to bring influence. We look too much like the culture around us.

Transitions come at the most inopportune times. They typically come when followers are in the midst of a struggle—when their energy is depleted and demands on them are high. Followers shouldn't be surprised that they have no time for a transition. There's never a "right" time for a transition.

MOTIVES

Radio commentator Paul Harvey has a favorite phrase that he uses when talking about news stories: "And now, the rest of the story."

The rest of the story about transitions is how God is going after the unseen issues that are often driving Christ-followers and Christian leaders. Avoidance of transitions often occurs because of the issues driving us surrounding that transition, and often throwing us off-course in our development.

I can be driven by ambition. Often, I'm unaware of it. What provides me fulfillment and fuels my service for God sometimes doesn't actually come from God. It comes from the need to perform and prove myself. Ambition and approval are my twin demons.

When I get into a transition, God goes after my motives. My own ideas and dreams can quickly become fuel for selfish fires. Facing that reality, however difficult, is an important truth that comes from the fires of a transition.

Much of the reason we refuse to slow down is related to our insecurities and the need to prove ourselves. These show up both in the Church and in the business world. Our motives and busyness are why we often don't get all of what God has for us in our transitions.

When you're tempted to skip or bail out of a transition, stop. Check yourself. Allow God to check your motives. Respond to God's processing during the transition, even when the timing may be wrong.

GOOD VERSUS BEST

The first time I ever heard someone talk about issues of good versus best, I was actually in a place I rarely go: a motivational seminar with Zig Ziglar. I'd never been to an event like that before.

I'd browsed through some of the books that ooze from the motivational world. None of them had impressed me. But during that night, in that lecture, I was challenged. I remember thinking about that idea for weeks. Was I involved in good things or best things? I thought about not letting my life go to that which was anything less than optimum contribution. I needed to surrender all again—to place everything at Jesus' disposal and ask Him what He thought of my focus.

The good can become the enemy of the best. This issue heightens during the mid-life years and, as such, is particularly an issue Baby Boomers now face. They've mastered the art of keeping all of their options open. Regardless of age or life situation, being distracted by the good is another reason for stumbling at the end.

Revisiting Ephesians 2:8-10 reminds us that each of us is a unique creation, destined to do good works. Those works have been woven into our lives before time began. They're seen in the fabric of our spiritual gifts, natural abilities, and acquired skills. At the moment you committed your life to become a Christ-follower, those works begin to surface. As you continue to journey with Christ, you'll need to fight through what you can do in order to find what you were made to do. That contribution becomes more evident as you go on.

Transitions touch hard issues. They'll revisit areas that have been dealt with before. And they'll cause Christ-followers to feel that they're out of control of the direction of their lives. God will do a new work that in the end will move a follower to greater fulfillment and meaning.

Christ-followers best discern their unique contribution in the context of Christian community. The problem is that many of those environments are toxic and dysfunctional. Too often, they're places where individuals refuse to take responsibility. Truth and change create a trap in which many Christ-followers get hurt. Nonetheless, a follower still needs to discern what God is doing during a transition in the context of community.

God uses transitions to help followers discover personal clarity and definition. Transitions "turn up the heat" to reveal new, breakthrough insights that help advance Christ-followers on to their unique and ultimate contribution. So, choose not to avoid times of transition, but to respond to God's greater, deeper work in your life.

UN-STUCK: APPLYING IT

Get all you can out of a transition. Resist the temptation to opt out. Allow God to go deeper into your life so that through your life He can go wider.

When a transition ends, you'll know it. The real question at the end of a transition isn't whether you've gone through one, but this: Has it gone through you?

What have you learned during your time of transition? How do you behave differently today from embracing the truths of past transitions?

In this chapter, we focused on ways to respond to a transition and putting yourself in a position of gaining all you can from your transition.

In the next chapter, we'll talk about the resolve that helps to facilitate an effective time of transition. A sovereign mindset is one such resolve.

18

resolve

The beginning of a path is always most important. Miss the entrance, and you will never walk the path. Perhaps the narrow gate that opens onto the route toward God, the gate that many Christian think they have walked but never have, can be found in an idea so simple that we often miss its force: You know you're finding God when you believe that God is good no matter what happens... We will know we have found God when nothing can shake our confidence in his unchanging goodness.

—LARRY CRABB, *FINDING GOD*

The three teenagers stood quietly by. Their choices had brought them to this moment, and their next choice would define their lives. But even before they decided, the choice had already been made. These three lived differently from the rest of their culture. They lived a life of resolve. And though their immediate fate would be placed in the hands of a vicious dictator, their minds were fixed and resolute, anchored in their sovereign God.

The confident stance of Shadrach, Meshach, and Abednego has impacted readers of all ages. They faced death with a bigger picture in mind. These three lived with a sovereign mindset—a mindset fixed on God.

Listen to their words: "King Nebuchadnezzar, we do not need to defend ourselves before you in this matter. If we are thrown into the blazing furnace, the God we serve is able to deliver us from it, and he will deliver us from Your Majesty's hand" (Daniel 3:16-17).

And it doesn't stop there. Their declaration wasn't just a belief that their God would save them. It was also a resolute stance that declared if their God didn't rescue them, they still wouldn't serve another king and his gods.

Compared to the situational approach to life today, these three represent an aberration. Their fixed resolve makes them seem like fanatics compared to us western Christians. Although many Christians around the world know this type of faith and resolve, it's an exception in our culture here in America. They stared death in the face and didn't flinch.

Why do we see so little of this type of resolve today? Where are the lives anchored in a resolve to follow God? Three teenagers had it back then. We need it today.

God uses transitions to build that kind of faith and resolve. They give Christ-followers a bird's eye view of a much bigger narrative and a much bigger God. One of the most important tools needed to process a transition is to approach a transition with a sovereign mindset—that is, to believe God is at work, designing, forming, and shaping a life destiny beyond what the eye can see.

SOVEREIGN MIND-SET

Mind-set (n) 1. A fixed mental attitude or disposition that predetermines a person's response to, and interpretations of, situations; 2. An inclination or habit.

Mindset became a term in the English language in the 1920s. A mindset is formed as a result of seeing life differently, either as a result of experience, education, prejudice, or event—or because of a viewpoint that predetermines a person's responses and interpretations of various situations.

A sovereign mindset believes that there is an ultimate, God-ordained purpose for our lives, whether seen or unseen. It believes that God is active, not passive. Regarding a Christ-follower's development, a sovereign mindset believes that God can use life to shape life. It believes that a Christ-follower can live a life of destiny. Each life in God's economy is part of an ultimate and grand narrative. It's about taking the deep theological truth of sovereignty and making it immensely practical.

Lives lived differently from the world inspire others. Within each Christ-follower is the potential for that kind of life. But to do so requires followers to process their transitions with a different mindset, one that acknowledges that God has the right to be God.

The life of a Christ-follower isn't about personal success, accomplishment, or even significance. It's about joining the larger story of redemption and living with a fixed resolve. This type of life can be lived now—it has been lived before. The cry of John the Baptist summarizes the goal of this life: "He must become greater; I must become less" (John 3:30).

Paul faced a series of transitions in his life and leadership. He lived through these with a fixed resolve about God's purposes and ultimate plan. This mindset enabled him to respond to faith challenges differently than others. From his early days in Antioch (Acts 11) to his dispatch by the church in Jerusalem to plant churches elsewhere (Acts 13) to his finishing well (2 Timothy), Paul witnessed the purposes of God lived out in his life.

So did Abraham. His life changed as God initiated his Awakening Transition and called him to leave all that he knew. To be given a son as a fulfillment of a promise, only to then be asked to sacrifice that son on a mountaintop altar, required a new level of trust in God's character. God shaped a deeper resolve and trust into Abraham as He transitioned his life and ministry. Developing a sovereign mindset isn't easy, but it's essential to the effective processing of your transitions.

RESOLVE

Adopting a strong sovereign mindset doesn't discount human responsibility. The reconciling of divine sovereignty and human responsibility is a question that has been asked throughout the history of the Church. Which camp is right on this issue? I submit that both are true.

Charles Spurgeon was once asked if he could reconcile the two truths of divine sovereignty and human responsibility. "I wouldn't try," he replied, "I never reconcile friends."

God is absolutely sovereign and He requires each of us to live fully responsible for our actions and obedience. Scripture is clear that God knows the future (Matthew 6:8; Psalm 139:1-4) and is in sovereign control of all things (Colossians 1:16-17; Daniel 4:35). The Bible is also clear that those who follow must also choose Him. God doesn't force us or cause us to do anything (James 1:13-14). Because of this, we're responsible for our own actions (Romans 3:19; 6:23; 9:19-21). How these facts work together may be impossible to fully reconcile, but true nonetheless (Romans 11:33-36).

Christians often distort these truths by either minimizing human responsibility in spiritual growth and service (Philippians 1:6; 4:13, 19) or overemphasizing God's absolute sovereignty in His right to rule and reign over the choices of humanity. Jesus has made it clear that without our abiding in Him and His abiding in us, there is no fruitfulness. We can do nothing apart from His works in and through those who "abide" in Him.

Adopting a fixed resolve and a sovereign mindset during your transition will provide insight into its four phases.

UN-STUCK: APPLYING IT

How's your resolve? It's one of the keys to getting all you can out of a transition. Consider the following questions:

- What clarity have you received about transitions after having worked through the concepts in this book?

- Are you headed toward a transition? What might work against your resolve? What do you need to remind yourself of as you begin to process your transition?

- Are you in a transition right now? What's working against your resolve? What needs to be addressed to help you stay the course? What assistance do you need to help you better process your transition?

Note: As you work through your transition, keep an eye on the Transition Life Cycle from chapter 4.

In this chapter, we focused on the resolve that puts Christ-followers into a position of gaining all they can from their transition.

In the next chapter, we'll talk about the willingness to relearn and go through the paradigm shifts that come as a result of a transition.

19

relearning

What comes into your mind when we think about God is the most important thing about us. The most significant fact about any man is not what he at a given time may say or do, but what he in his deep heart conceives God to be like.

—A. W. TOZER, *THE KNOWLEDGE OF THE HOLY*

It is not enough that we behave better; we must come to see reality differently. We must learn to see the depths of things, not just reality at a superficial level.

—WILLIAM H. SHANNON, *SILENCE ON FIRE*

So why does God choose this way to shape His followers? Perhaps more closely examining exactly what occurs during transitions will shed some light on these matters.

PARADIGM SHIFTS

Transitions break Christ-followers free from old patterns and plateau in their growth. At the core of transitions is a shift in one's thinking and lifestyle. Transitions often represent a shift in one's paradigm.

Paradigm shifts cause an individual to utilize the same information and facts in new ways. Paradigm shifts provide new ideas and ways to overcome obstacles in the midst of change. A paradigm shift pushes Christ-followers to see and do life in new ways.

Paradigm shifts that occur during a transition break unhealthy behavior. They create fresh and new truth to invade recurring problems. New approaches to life often mean new contexts for living.

God has always used paradigm shifts and transitions to shape the lives of those whom He desires to influence. Consider a few examples:

- **Job:** a major shift in viewing the nature of suffering (Job 1:20)

- **Jonah:** a major shift in viewing how God looks at non-Jews (Jonah 3:33)

- **Habakkuk:** a major shift in a leader's view of God (Habakkuk 3:19)

- **John the Baptist:** a major shift concerning the person and work of Jesus (John 1:32)

Nicodemus also experienced a dramatic paradigm shift. His nighttime meeting with Jesus was the key paradigm shift: Jesus arrived and turned upside-down much of what Nicodemus had believed about the coming of the Messiah. This transition shifted his beliefs and convictions forever. It was a high-risk, life-altering paradigm shift that would propel his life in a new direction.

The following verses document Nicodemus's encounter with Christ and the resulting shift in his paradigm:

- John 3:3: "Very truly I tell you, no one can see the kingdom of God unless they are born again." Jesus here is calling for a major shift in Nicodemus's knowledge base—that is, the basis by which he relates to God.

- John 3:5: "Very truly I tell you, no one can enter the kingdom of God unless they are born of water and the Spirit." Going through this paradigm shift will require a new direction spiritually from within and the regeneration that is a work of God's Spirit.

- John 3:7: "You should not be surprised at my saying, 'You must be born again.'" This unique experience is about being aligned with the true Messiah and a shift to live your life as part of His Kingdom. When you've moved beyond this paradigm shift, the result will be confirmed.

Paradigm shifts can bring insight in four areas:

1. New insights about God and His character

2. New ways that God desires deeper faith and trust in Himself

3. Insights about how God is at work and what this means to life direction

4. What God now desires in terms of personal change in the interior life and exterior ministry of a Christ-follower

In a transition, paradigm shifts are used to move a Christ-follower to a deeper understanding of his or her unique life contribution. Four types of paradigm shifts often occur during times of transitions.

SHIFTS IN ROLE CLARITY

God moves followers into different environments of influence. More than a job change, God purposes these changes to shape lives of impact. He uses the context in which He places a follower as a way to begin to surface his or her contribution.

Role has to do with contribution, as well as clarifying what Christ-followers deposit in each setting in which they find themselves. Paradigm shifts occur as Christ-followers use their abilities, spiritual gifts, and skills to influence others toward God's purposes.

Whether you're in the marketplace or serve as a full-time Christian worker, you must be open to gaining a new understanding of your unique role. God places Christ-followers into a variety of environments as a way of helping them better define their contribution.

SHIFTS IN SELF-KNOWLEDGE

Self-definition is essential to better understanding one's unique contribution in life. God gives confidence to a Christ-follower through insights gained during a transition.

Transitions propel a Christ-follower to look within and resolve issues that often cloud self-understanding. Challenge of an individual's worth, personal development, and views of God can all provoke new levels of growth that otherwise might not happen as a result of a shift in paradigms.

Transitions of this type also help individuals better understand how they relate to others, including a tendency to over-rely on others for approval for their own self-acceptance. Coming to terms with one's self promotes greater health and a new awareness of God's true love and acceptance.

SHIFTS IN PASSION CLARITY

Each Christ-follower's contribution is an unique mix of that person's gifts and core passions. Together, these produce a unique set of methods and ways to contribute.

Transitions of this type bring to the surface core passions that in some cases hadn't been known previously. They also help to clarify motivation and begin to sort through ongoing frustrations. Issues of passion play an important role in future decision-making about life direction.

SHIFTS IN NEW KNOWLEDGE

Transitions and the corresponding paradigm shift bring with them new knowledge. They help Christ-followers acquire new information and new ways of thinking. These transitions cause Christ-followers to see change differently. A breakthrough in this arena can also be used to grant new spiritual authority to a Christ-follower.

But knowledge transitions also can create tension. They can rub up against convictions and reveal complacency, irritating the status quo. New cognitive growth can take followers to new places in their spiritual maturity. Some can misinterpret knowledge transitions as compromise. The in-between time often can be a lonely journey. It takes followers to places previously unknown.

Most people take little time to look at their lives, and even less time examining their lives from God's perspective. Most people become trapped by life itself. Transitions force a Christ-follower to take the "big view" of his or her life and choices.

Something unique occurs between God and a Christ-follower in a transition. The follower encounters God and His character in a new way and he or she begins to relearn the ways and reasoning of God. Because of this, paradigm shifts also create deeper interior growth in a Christ-follower.

INTIMACY

Transitions call followers deeper. They challenge them to go to new places in the journey of "trust" and "loss of control." Paradigm shifts occur concerning God's character. Sometimes Christ-followers are brought face-to-face with apparent contradictions about God:

- How is all this pain and uncertainty loving?

- Where is God's promise of power and provision?

- If He's good, why is He silent?

- If I'm honoring God, why does my business (or my church) continue to fail?

- How could He command us to go someplace new and then not provide for our needs?

- What is the purpose of all my brokenness and failure?

- Why is life so hard?

Unless a transition occurs, committed Christ-followers shut down the real questions of life. But God wants to be asked these questions. These and other questions open the door to discovery. God invites us into the "mystery"—that is, the mystery of who He is and how He can be entrusted with our lives.

PERSPECTIVE

Transitions build ownership of one's future direction. Through discovery, God sheds new insight on life and its purpose. Examination and self-discovery impart maturity into a follower's life.

Scripture is filled with moments where servants of God confront the need for a change in perspective. A classic example is Elisha's servant seeing the reality of the spiritual battle (2 Kings 6:8-23).

Christ-followers too often appraise things "logically" and miss the truth of a situation. Transitions force a follower to see struggles and challenges from an eternal, godly perspective.

Transitions call a follower to go back, assess what has transpired in past chapters, resolve conflicts, and bring about necessary reconciliation—making them better able to move forward unhindered. Sins of the past are less likely to be repeated and passed on to the next generation because of transitions.

God also initiates a transition to bring emotional perspective and closure to past patterns of behavior. Past hurts and struggles often arrest a follower's development, yet confronting the past often brings resistance. However, the purpose of looking back, even at the most difficult moments, is not to stay in the past, but to experience the release needed for the future.

UNIQUENESS

Each Christ-follower is "fearfully and wonderfully made" (Psalm 139:14). A follower's life is shaped for a specific contribution (Ephesians 2:10). We each carry a unique, spiritual shape that has been engineered by God not to be buried, but lived. Each Christ-follower carries an individualized DNA that is more than just our physical life script.

Transitions call for alignment with our God-ordained uniqueness. What distinguishes our lives from a robotic view of life is that followers share in the responsibility for their development by making right choices. The responsibility to choose does not rule out an absolute sovereign Creator God. (For more on this, go back and review chapter 3.)

UN-STUCK: APPLYING IT

Transitions develop Christ-followers, pointing them to a unique and ultimate contribution.

- What from this chapter has resonated with you?

- What has God called you to re-learn during your transitions?

- How have you applied this learning?

- How do you believe God is at work in the midst of your transition?

In this chapter, we focused on the paradigm shifts and changes that often come as a result of a transition.

In the next and final chapter, we'll talk about moving forward to what God has prepared you to be and do for His glory.

20

next

So I am like Nicodemus, who came by night, said safe things about Jesus to his colleagues, and expressed his guilt by bringing to the grave more myrrh and aloes than needed or desired. Nicodemus deserves all my attention. Can I stay a Pharisee and follow Jesus too?

—HENRI NOUWEN, *THE ROAD TO DAYBREAK*

As I write this book, I'm suspended on the trapeze bar high above the crowd. My fingers are beginning to feel the pressure of release. I'm feeling the fear of the unknown. I must believe in the hands of the catcher in order to discover and live out my ultimate contribution.

I'm at the moment of the release. Having climbed the ladder and having launched out away from the platform, I've experienced a life and ministry I never thought possible. I now face the biggest challenge of my life. I'm called to believe that as I step out again, His hands are there ready for the catch.

When I was younger, I scoffed at older leaders who failed to seize and act on new opportunities. I now understand their reluctance. I'm staring at the Deciding Transition. This transition has meant moving beyond the organization I've served with for the past 20 years. My focus has tightened as God narrows me to the role of coaching and resourcing breakthrough in the lives of risk-taking leaders. My new venture is called Leader Breakthru. Our motto is, "Resourcing and coaching breakthrough in the lives of risk-taking, Kingdom leaders."

But it's more than that. It's also the transition to my ultimate contribution. Leaders from all around the world are in need of breakthroughs in their leadership and personal development. As they develop others, they themselves hunger for a resource for their own development. I want to be of help.

And yet, as the bar swings back and forth, I feel the panic of letting go. I have friends and a sense of being known in the organization I'm leaving. Although I've played the pioneer and innovator role in my life, I feel both the exhilaration and the sheer terror of starting over again.

I trust God, but how much?

Will He be there to catch me?

I've believed it for others, but do I truly believe it for myself and my family?

FROM DOING TO BEING

The Entry, Evaluation, and Surrender Phases of this transition haven't been easy. They've already taken two long years. Organizational change has taken its toll on a leader. The further I've gone, the more I've experienced detachment from the vision, people, and things I once held dear. I feel both isolation and pain. I desperately want to project my fears and struggles onto the organization I leave, but in the end I know that God himself is repositioning me for the endgame.

Looking back, I can see my two earlier major life transitions. In my mid 30s, I made a major life direction course change by stepping away from a pastoral position to join an organization and lead a team to Australia. That transition was difficult, but exhilarating. I climbed up the trapeze ladder with both terror and a thrill in my heart. That transition meant a major geographical move and uprooting my young family. And yet these proved to be some of the most fruitful years of my life.

This Awakening Transition set a new course direction for me. My life calling began to unfold. I was now helping lost or discouraged leaders and churches discover their Christ-designed destiny. I was helping reposition churches and organizations to better impact the world. I had no idea what that all meant. I simply knew that somehow I was living out God's unique design for my life. Because of the needs that this new challenge presented, God provided me with my most significant life mentor along with a set of new paradigms, skills, methods, and relationships to carry it all out.

My second major life transition occurred in my mid-40s. This was a time of leaving the security of the platform. I was being led to create a system that could empower facilitators to impart strategic changes to local churches. This push away from the platform led again to a flurry of new activity and effort. This new program was based upon our past work, but required a new level of faith. We assembled a work team, staged events, wrote new materials, and engaged church leaders and their churches in a new process called ReFocusing.

This period of my life was also a time of spiritual growth and renewal. God taught me things and took me to places I'd never dreamed of earlier in my life. Fruit was harvested, leaders were encouraged, and new resources were developed. During this period, I also went through several changes in my organizational assignment.

In my early 50s, I took a new assignment within the organization. I knew it was important and needed to be done, but I soon recognized that this new role simply wasn't for me. I repositioned a major division, yet longed to return to working with leaders, creating new resources, and pioneering new systems. A small step toward my passion area of leadership development led to a sense of God saying, "This is what I've made you for."

However, I also realized that I'd need freedom and open territory to explore new ground. In the end, I would need a new vehicle, not because the former one was bad, but because the new one would give me the freedom necessary to explore this new terrain.

This brought me to a decision: should I stay or should I let go? I made the decision to let go of all that I had known for the last 20 years and to trust in the way God had shaped my life and contribution.

Reluctant finger by reluctant finger, my grip has been pried loose. I now must move beyond the comfort and camaraderie of the past and believe in the "catcher" God, as well as what He has designed for my life. It's a new defining moment for me.

FAITH CHALLENGE

Imagine that moment (maybe you're there right now) of being suspended after letting go and before being caught. Close your eyes and imagine a high-flying artist who has released the bar high above and been flung headlong into the air. Watch the eyes of this acrobat now passionately focused on identifying the approaching catcher.

This moment is a mixture of excitement, anxiety, concentration, fear, loss of control, hope, uncertainty, and incredible aloneness. And then, as if out of nowhere, swinging in obscurity is the silhouette of another. Imagine the catch and the grasp of strong arms attaching to your forearms as if they had never been apart.

The dust from the chalk on the trapeze bar begins to disappear, revealing the rescuer, your true friend, the one who said He would never turn or leave you or forsake the call He had placed on your life. Could there be anything greater than that moment?

This is the moment in life when Christ-followers hear the words they've longed their whole lives to hear: "Well done, good and faithful servant." Will you hear those words? Will you finish well? It's possible, and God will use transitions to help get you there.

You can finish well. You can hear those words mentioned above. It's been said that few leaders actually finish well. I'll make you a deal: I'll meet you there!

UN-STUCK: APPLYING IT

Did you get all that you can out of your study of transitions? Finishing this book doesn't mean your transition is done. Here are a few steps for moving forward:

- Return to the Transition Life Cycle (chapter 4) and the three key transitions (chapter 10) as your key navigational tools.

- Continue to process your transition with the help of a coach or mentor.

(Note: For further assistance, Leader Breakthru offers transition coaching: www.leaderbreakthru.com/coach-me)

Appendix A:
Small Group Discussion Guide

This book has been designed to be used as a small group discussion resource. Reviewing Stuck! as a group often provides help and encouragement by hearing the insights of others who are also experiencing a time of transition.

This small group guide has been designed to provide you with a format to review in a group setting over four sessions.

Stuck! can also be used for an eight session small group study by expanding chapters 8-10, 11 and 12, 13 and 14, and 15 and 16 into separate times of discussion.

HOW COULD IT WORK?

Easy. *Stuck!* has four major sections. Each provides a theme for discussion and interaction. Four interaction times will provide insight into the purpose and pathway through a transition.

The four major sections of the book are as follows:

- Definitions and Characteristics (chapters 1–4)

- Four Stages (chapters 5–9)

- Three Defining Moments (chapters 10–16)

- Where to From Here? (chapters 17–20)

In the following pages, you'll find an introduction and overview of the four sections, as well as discussion questions found in the chapters to help promote greater insight and application.

SECTION 1: DEFINITION AND CHARACTERISTICS (CHAPTERS 1–4)

In chapters 1–4, *Stuck!* surfaces the reality and nature of a transition. Transitions occur in the life of every Christ-follower. The issue isn't whether transitions occur, but rather recognizing and processing the transitions we'll each experience.

The temptation is to deny or take a shortcut through a transition (chapter 1). Transitions produce some of the most important insights and lessons each of us can learn in life (chapter 2). The question of "why" haunts many Christ-followers as they face the confusion and isolation that often accompany a transition (chapter 3). The good news is that there's a way through a transition. The Transition Life Cycle provides a template that transitions often take (chapter 4).

Review the discussion questions from chapters 1–4 listed below. Pick the questions that most relate to your current experience, or ones that most interest the group. As you discuss the issues, look for patterns and themes on the feelings that surround a transition.

During one of Israel's darkest moments, Jeremiah spoke important truths —truths also relevant and important for God's followers today. Read Jeremiah 29. What insights do you see? What are the promises?

Real Life (chapter 1)

How would you describe the last few months of your journey with God? Spend some time journaling about what has been occurring. Describe what you have felt and what you deem important. Identify some key words that characterize what's going on. Is there an intuitive sense that there's something more going on than just a difficult time?

Different (chapter 2)

Processing your transitions. Knowing yourself. Living differently. Most do little in terms of thinking about past life and development. Think of a time of transition in your life. Retrieve it from your memory bank. What happened? What was different about yourself as a result?

Why? (chapter 3)

Why a transition is occurring is often not discerned until after it's over. However, try to answer these questions about a current or recent transition:

- Why did God choose to push the pause button in your journey?

- Why now?

- What is it that He might be trying to address? Add? Affirm? Adjust?

The Life Cycle (chapter 4)

Are you in a transition?

- If so, when did it begin?

- Where do you think you are in the cycle?

- What have you been remembering about the past?

- What has God been saying to you?

- What issues seem to be surfacing?

- What has been your response?

SECTION 2: FOUR STAGES (CHAPTERS 5–9)

There are typically a series of stages as a transition progresses. Often, Christ-followers don't realize they're in a transition until it's well under way. The hurt, isolation, or confusion that can accompany the beginning of a transition makes it difficult to see. Typically, those experiencing the beginning of a transition are just trying to cope or survive (chapter 5).

Once the dust settles, and the transition is acknowledged, a time of evaluation and questioning begins. Why? Where is God in all of this? What went wrong? Where is all of this leading? Why has God gone silent? What is He trying to teach me? (chapter 6).

Life with Christ is about trust. The challenges and the struggles we each face reveal a greater need to trust God. Transitions lead to times of surrender and increased dependency on Christ. The surrender of control must be revisited. As a Christ-follower yields, again, to the "author and finisher of the faith," God begins a deeper and wider work in His children (chapter 7).

The call to align with God and His work, and the prize of surrender to that work, is fresh insight and truth. God reveals His designs and His plans. The nation of Israel most embodies this truth. As they yielded to God, He revealed His purposes and their unique destiny. For more on this, see Jeremiah 29 (chapter 9).

Review the discussion questions from chapters 5-9 listed below. Pick those that most relate to your current experience, or ones that most interest the group.

As you discuss the topics, consider how do the four stages apply to your current situation. If you're in a transition right now, where are you in the journey?

Look at the chronology of Peter's final days with Christ (John 18-21). Are there any aspects of a transition or the Transition Life Cycle in these verses?

Confusion (chapter 5)

What if you realize that you're at the Entry Phase of a transition? What should you do?

Discuss the following:

- Wait. If you're truly in a time of transition, it will unfold.

- Adopt a posture of openness. Instead of seeking to end or remedy your struggles, open up to what God might be doing in your life.

- Start a journal. Write down your thoughts about where you are. List the issues that you find yourself pondering. What are your questions?

- Reflect on the issues that you believe launched you into the transition. What's the nature of those issues? Why are they so difficult?

- Ask God to begin to reveal His purposes, even in the midst of your hurt and confusion. Pray and reflect by asking, "Lord, what are you at work doing?"

- Find someone to travel alongside you. This shouldn't be someone who claims to have all the answers, but someone committed to help you process your questions.

The Waterline (chapter 6)

Most likely, evaluation will produce moments of truth when a follower comes face-to-face with issues of self. Evaluation often produces an incredible need for God and a re-encounter with the love and grace of God.

- What has surfaced now as you think through the Evaluation Phase of a transition? What have you learned to value as a result?

- Look back at the four categories of questions. Apply them to your current transition and evaluate what led up to it.

- What makes you feel stuck? What is God going after? If you could address one issue right now, what would it be?

Alignment (chapter 7)

The prize of surrender is revelation. Most want revelation. Few want surrender. Look at the four obstacles again. Which of these could keep you from surrender?

- Strong ego (self-sufficiency)

- Shame or guilt (past struggles)

- Lack of self-acceptance (accepting God's grace and love)

- High achievement (task-focused)

Don't get stuck in the Alignment Phase; your future depends on it! Lay down anything that may be keeping your stuck here.

Letting Go (chapter 8)

Sacred space is more than just a different spin on having a devotional time with God. Creating sacred space has to do with intentional time to wait and recognize that "still small voice." Which of these need intentional focus to help you better discern God's call on your life?

- Meditating on the heart of psalms

- Reflection and time of journaling

- Listening: the capacity to be quiet before God

- Ability to discern what's next and responding to God's leading

Don't run past the need to create sacred space, and letting go of the past in order to move into the future.

Living Forward (chapter 9)

Have you heard God speak? That may feel like a daunting experience. Let's process what might be occurring. What does God seem to be saying? What's the breakthrough? List the experiences where you sensed God speaking to you in new ways. How does what you're hearing line up with the following:

- Scripture?

- Your past?

- Counsel from those who know you best?

SECTION 3: THREE DEFINING MOMENTS (CHAPTERS 10–16)

Some transitions are bigger in nature and importance than others. Christ-followers will go through several transitions, but there are three major transitions that occur en route to a Christ-follower finishing well. These three work a follower to the potential moment of convergence, where individuals discover their unique contribution (chapter 10).

The Awakening Transition is about calling. It's the moment when decisions are made about life's direction and purpose. Questions about direction tend to be predominant. The problem is that answers are less evident (chapters 11 and 12).

The Deciding Transition is when an individual begins to face the need for prioritization and a decision-making grid. With multiple demands, and the scarcity of time, Christ-followers must discern how to say "no" if they are to say "yes" to God's plans and design (chapters 13 and 14).

The Finishing Transition is about completing the race set before a Christ-follower. Finishing is about focusing on one's unique contribution and legacy, as well as the life imprint one leaves behind (chapters 15 and 16).

Chapters 12, 14, and 16 are unique in that they're comprised of a series of coaching questions that can serve as the basis for discussion and interaction. Pick the chapter that most relates to your current transition, or interests your group, and process it in a deeper way.

Read through the dialogue between the coach and those experiencing the transition. What's helpful? How does the advice apply to your situation? What questions or thoughts do you still have?

Reflect on the lives of, Daniel, Timothy, and Paul. These three lives help illustrate these three transitions. What do they tell us about the results of going through these defining moments? What lessons can we learn? Look at Hebrews 13:7-8 and note the exhortation to study the lives of other leaders.

SECTION 4: WHERE TO FROM HERE? (CHAPTERS 17–20)

Dr. J. Robert Clinton makes this comment about transitions: "Get everything that God has for you out of each of the transitions He brings to you."

As we've discussed, there's a temptation to:

- Become preoccupied with life and its many demands

- Want answers prematurely

- Want answers more than intimacy with God

Resist and lean into the difficult. There are insights hidden in a transition (chapter 17). It'll take resolve and a commitment to live out the trust you profess to have in God. But if you're going to move from one phase of your development to the next, you must go through (not around) your transitions. Put your energy and passion into deeper intimacy with Christ and living a life that counts (chapter 18).

One of the key results of a transition is a major shift in one's paradigm. God changes how we view life and the obstacles we face. New perspective breeds new courage and hope. Transitions reveal the need for change and help to give insight into the way forward in one's thinking and life (chapter 19).

Transitions aren't without risk. They will require us to leave the comfortable, take the unknown path, and set out into the promised. There's a path and a way forward. Up ahead is the prize. Not big numbers or famous recognition, but that moment when an individual realizes, "for this I was born" (chapter 20).

Response (chapter 17)

Choose to lean into your transition and get all you can from this in-between time in your development. Your response to your transition matters.

- What could cause you to short circuit your transition?

- What are the reasons you might rush ahead, and not get all you can?

- What happens to you when God calls on you to wait on Him, and not rush ahead?

- Why is it hard for you to wait?

Resolve (chapter 18)

How's your resolve? It's one of the keys to getting all you can out of a transition.

- What clarity have you received about transitions after having interacted with the concepts in this book?

- Are you headed toward a transition? What might work against your resolve? What do you need to remind yourself of as you begin to process your transition?

- Are you in a transition right now? What's working against your resolve? What needs to be addressed to help you stay the course? What assistance do you need to help you better process your transition?

Relearning (chapter 19)

Understanding that God works and uses transitions to develop His followers brings purpose to the toughest of moments and gives purpose to living in a time of the almost, but not yet.

- What has resonated with you from this chapter as we've discussed the reasons for transitions?

- Do you simply want to skip ahead and move on?

- Have you taken control yourself and locked out the ways God might be at work?

- Do you believe God is truly at work in the midst of your transition?

- How is your struggle in trusting God with control right now?

Next (chapter 20)

Did you get all you can out of your study of transitions?

- Use the Transition Life Cycle (chapter 4) and the three key transitions (chapter 10) as your key navigational tools.

- Continue to process your transition with the help of a coach or mentor.

Note: Leader Breakthru offers transition coaching: www.leaderbreakthru.com.

Appendix B:
Boundary Processing

Below are excerpts from an article by Dr. J. Robert Clinton entitled, "Looking at Critical Transition Times in Leader's Lives."

Every leader goes through critical times of transition in his or her ministry. The key to these times is to put them into the perspective of a lifetime of development. Looked at directly, with the narrow focus of the now, the events of the present, they can be overwhelming and discouraging. We can feel like giving up, backing out of leadership altogether. But placed in the context of a lifetime of development, they can be seen to serve at least four major purposes.

First, they deepen one's relationship to God.

Second, they bring closure to recent experiences—that is, we learn lessons concerning the situation that has catapulted us into the boundary time. We make amends in terms of our inner life, recognizing the need for forgiveness and reconciliation, where we can. We put that time behind us with a sense of having gained as much positive from it as we can.

Third, they expand our perspectives to see new things. We may be released to consider something new and different that we otherwise would never have opted for. We may be taken to a new level of realization of our God-given potential.

Finally, they cause us to make decisions that will launch us into a new aspect of ministry, or a new ministry altogether, or a new phase of development. These boundary times are times of confusion, turmoil, sometimes pain, and almost ways reflection with uncertain resolution. They last anywhere from two or three months to as long as six years.

There is a pattern to them:

- The entry stage and its characteristic backward reflection: a seeking to understand what has happened to bring about the boundary.

- The evaluation stage and its characteristic upward reflection: the drawing of God to see the meta goals behind the whole process, the deepening of relationship with the sovereign God.

- The termination stage with its characteristic forward look: decisions are made with a confidence, even though the details are not always clear, that God is moving one forward with excitement to a new time of expansion, purpose, and release. Forewarned is forearmed! Getting perspective on what happens in these boundary times before they happen can make the difference in how we respond in them.

THE BIG PICTURE: A FRAMEWORK FOR BOUNDARY THINKING

Boundaries imply transition from something to something. We need a bigger picture than just the present if we are to talk about boundaries. One important tool for getting this larger perspective is the ministry timeline, which was developed in leadership emergence theory. A leader's life, when viewed as a whole, can usually be broken up into major time periods. These time periods are called development phases. Smaller time periods within *development phases* are called *sub-phases.*

Comparative studies of leader's lives have resulted in a generalized overall timeline that can serve as a backdrop for evaluating a leader's unique timeline. It also helps us define the notion of boundary. Note the major phases (designated by Roman numerals) in the following illustration. Now note the sub-phases, which are designated by capital letters. These are the time periods that help us pinpoint what boundaries are.

The Ministry Timeline & Ministry Philosophy Variables			
Phase I	Phase II	Phase III	Phase IV
Ministry Foundations	General Ministry	Focused Ministry	Convergent Ministry
A.　　　　B.	A.　　　B.　　　C.	A.　　　B.	A.　B.　C.
---- B1 ----	--- B2 ---	---- B3 ----	

THE MINISTRY TIME-LINE

The times shown for each sub-phase are general and represent a range of times observed in people's lives. For example, a typical leader coming from a Christian heritage might have a foundational sub-phase lasting about 18 years. The transition into leadership may take about 6 years. General Ministry involving three or four major ministry assignments may last about 10 years until competency is reached. Focused Ministry may last 12 years before there is movement into a unique ministry with a role that fits the leader's gifts and experiences.

So, our average leader would be about 55 years old before moving into convergence. In general, boundary times represent those times of movement from one phase to another as indicated by [B1].

There can also be a lesser boundary time within a sub-phase, which is not shown above. That more minor transition would be a significant change of ministry assignment within a given sub-phase. Of course, more boundary times could be designated for the above timeline. There are boundaries between each of the phases and sub-phases and several in the sub-phases.

BOUNDARY TIME

A boundary time represents that period of time around a boundary point characterized by:

- activity that signals to the leader that some major change is coming,

- activity that releases the leader from the previous time period or focus,

- activity that draws the leader to recognize divine intervention, and

- activity that involves response on the leader's part to the intervention and toward the new time or focus.

This extended time around a boundary point illustrates the complexity involved in defining a boundary and leads us to a helpful definition.

Hans Finzel (1988) made a comparative study of major boundary processes of historical characters, as well as contemporary characters. Finzel's research not only identified processes related to the boundary time, but a three-stage pattern covering a boundary time. The diagram on the next page depicts the three-stage pattern and gives a comprehensive overview of what can happen during an extended boundary.

OVERALL PATTERN: THREE STAGES

Looking at the boundary as a whole there are three stages:

1. The Entry Stage

2. The Evaluation Stage

3. The Termination Stage

Of course, in shorter boundaries, like a true boundary point, these activities might collapse and merge and all of them might not be there. But, on the whole, they describe, tentatively predict, and help one assess where and what is happening in a boundary.

Note the crucial points involved in the stages: initiating activity, turning point, and resolution. The processes (15 process items—e.g. conflict, crises, etc.) are arranged time-wise where they most likely occur. Arrows indicate the range over which these process items might occur.

Often prior to and sometimes concurrent with the *Entry Stage* is some sort of initiating activity that begins to move a leader into the boundary. Common activities are the negative items of *Turmoil* and *Guidance* including conflict, crisis, life crisis, and negative preparation. Occasionally other guidance activities such as divine contact or sovereign guidance will propel a leader into a boundary. Change of perspective, such as a paradigm shift and a new ministry structure insight, will cause a leader to enter a boundary. This is especially so as the outworking of the perspective brings dissonance in the present ministry situation.

After entrance into a boundary, there is the major focus, which looks backward and reflects on what has happened. Frequently, if the boundary involves negative items, there is the attempt to vindicate and defend one's own thinking, behavior, and leadership. The entry stage is dominated by retrospective reflection and a questioning spirit.

Once solidly entrenched in the boundary, there is a shift toward an inward assessment—that is, seeking to learn the lessons from what has happened. This signals movement into Stage 2, the *Evaluation Stage*. The burden is now less on blaming or vindicating and more on what can be learned and how it will affect the leadership character, skills, and values of the leader experiencing the boundary processing. Frequently, the leader is in some isolation experience, either externally imposed and not by choice or by choice. A training interlude is often a self-choice isolation experience that characterizes the evaluation stage.

During this early part of Stage 2, the leader is frequently drawn closer to God. There is the desire for God to meet the leader in the situation. This movement from a backward look or focus to an *upward focus* is a major change in the leader in terms of learning response and is usually preparation for the major activity of boundary processing, the turning point. The turning point is the pivotal activity of all lengthy boundary processing. It is the point at which there is change from a retrospective and inward focus on self, and the previous experience, to an external and forward look at the next ministry that is coming. To use the tunnel analogy, it is when the light in the tunnel is now ahead and not behind.

A leadership committal is often the culminating experience that signals the turning point. The upward focus on God and deepening relationship often is part of God's activity to bring about a new level of surrender for ministry. That surrender might be accompanied by a destiny revelation experience or some sovereign guidance experience or new ministry structure insight. All of these give added clarity about what might happen in the future. After the turning point, the major focus is *looking forward* to the upcoming development phase and not upward or backward.

Isolation processing or training progress processing which frequently accompanies Stage 2, (the Evaluation Stage), will usually continue into Stage 3, (the Termination Stage), and will help in the decision-making process, which is looking toward the future. Guidance items also frequently help shape the future decisions. Stage 3, the *Termination Stage*, is concerned with the decisions that will terminate the boundary and resolve the situation. Once these decisions are made, the boundary is terminated. However, the outworking of the decisions and the early part of the upcoming development may still feel like part of the boundary.

This description gives a framework for understanding boundary processing, whether phase, sub-phase, or minor, that an individual leader goes through in his or her unique development. The next section looks at the ministry timeline, that generic comparative timeline, and seeks to point out some of the specific boundaries and characteristics of them.

BOUNDARY PROCESSING

Boundary processing represents the activity taking place during a boundary time, which functions:

- to initiate the boundary;

- to shape the leader's thinking about the previous time period, including learning lessons about self, ministry, and relationships to others;

- to give guidance to the leader;

- to deepen the relationship of the leader to God; and

- to bring a psychological and spiritual release from the past time period so as to move toward the new with anticipation.

Certain incidents in our lives are used by God to shape us in various ways to give us leadership values, to teach us leadership lessons, to form character, and to instill deep convictions. In leadership emergence theory, we label these incidents as process incidents. Process incidents are the actual occurrences from a given life of those providential events, people, circumstances, special divine intervention, inner-life lessons, or other like items. God uses these to develop a person by shaping leadership character, leadership skills, and leadership values. A comparative study of like process incidents across many lives has led to the defining of special categories of incidents, which we label as process items. A process item is a label inductively drawn from a comparative analysis of process incidents, which categorizes incidents into groups with like properties and functions. Process items, when studied across lives, help us recognize and even suggest the kinds of values that will arise from these life experiences.

Any process item, if it is sensed as a special intervention from God, causes serious reflection. Usually lessons are learned from this. The accumulation of these lessons over a lifetime builds up the set of values that comprise a ministry philosophy. The lessons can deal with our relationship to God, character and personal ethics, practical ministry guidelines, ministry ethics, guidance, destiny, and other factors suited uniquely to the individual. While all process items teach lessons that develop us as leaders, the process items that occur in boundary times are especially important since they are taken collectively. They move us forward in guidance toward our place in God's destiny.

Finzel (1988) identified major process items that were common to most of the lives of these leaders. His study, plus more recent analysis, has resulted in the following list of important boundary processes.

Fifteen kinds of processing items associated with boundary activity are listed below.

BOUNDARY ACTIVITY 1: TURMOIL

1. Conflict:

    - Personal inner turmoil (spiritual, emotional, restlessness, etc.)

    - Relational turmoil (interpersonal problems)

    - Ministry oriented turmoil (factions, differences in philosophy, etc.)

2. Crisis:

    - Macro contextual (war, other external disasters)

    - Threat of termination of ministry

3. Life Crisis:

    - Life-threatening pressure

    - Pressures that cause deep reflection on the meaning of life and ultimate purposes

BOUNDARY ACTIVITY 2: RADICAL

4. Leadership Renewal Experience:

    - A time in which there is a change—a fresh committal to God in terms of a new ministry venture God is directing toward

5. Paradigm Shift:

    - The breakthrough by God that instills a new perspective affecting the leader's thought and activity

6. Ministry Structure:

- A special kind of paradigm shift that involves learning something about how to deliver one's ministry more effectively

BOUNDARY ACTIVITY 3: GENERAL

7. Isolation:

- A setting aside from ministry by God for growth and deepening of relationship

- A shift forward to ministering out of being rather than doing

- A focus on being rather than doing

8. Training Progress:

- The completion of a significant training experience (whether formal, non-formal, or informal) that affects leadership skills and values so as to alter future ministry

BOUNDARY ACTIVITY 4: FUTURE

9. Faith Challenge:

- A discerning that God is calling toward an expansion

- A new or particular step of faith that must be taken

- A frightening challenge about trusting God beyond one's comfort zone

10. Ministry Challenge:

- A discerning that God is calling one toward a new or expanded ministry assignment

11. Influence-mix:

- A discerning that God is expanding the challenge
  sphere of influence—either the direct face-to-face influence (extensiveness, comprehensiveness, intensiveness), the indirect (media, relational), or organizational (networking, power groups)

BOUNDARY ACTIVITY 5: GUIDANCE

12. Divine Contact:

- The perceived intervention of God via some person at a critical time with information that is timely, encouraging, opportunistic, and clarifying

13. Destiny Revelation:

- The breaking in of God in an unusual way to reveal or clarify next steps or future ministry so as to instill a sense of destiny and renewed hope in serving God

14. Negative Preparation:

- The accumulative perception that a series of happenings involving people, events, etc. are being used by God for more than character processing—they are actually being used by God to release someone from their present situation and give them a positive desire for the next situation

15. Additional Sovereign Processing:

- The unusual breaking in of God to give guidance via confirming circumstances, direct revelation, etc.

THE OVERALL EFFECT OF A BOUNDARY: THE BOUNDARY TASK

A boundary task represents an overall thrust, a summary statement of what God was basically accomplishing during a boundary time, which is usually only evaluated some time after the fact by retrospective reflection.

This final boundary term is a strategic one and not so easily grasped. It requires a broader view of a life that can put a boundary in context of the bigger picture. In retrospect, one can look back at a boundary time that has been completed in the past. Usually when considered as a whole, one or two major things will usually be identified as having been accomplished by God during the boundary period as a whole.

In order to see this, one has to know where they were in development before the boundary and where they are in development after the boundary. Typically, this understanding of development needs almost a whole development phase of time after the boundary in order to be appreciated. Identification of boundary tasks instills confidence that God is working in the life.

ARTICLE SUMMARY

This article examines one aspect of perspective that is crucial to the overall development of a leader: crucial times of transition. Leaders can transition from one ministry assignment to another, from one ministry to another, or from one phase of their life to another. Each of these transitions involves thresholds of a kind. They vary in time—some being as short as a few months, others lasting as long as six years.

This paper will examine these transitions, called boundaries. It will define the notion of boundary in general and three kinds in specific.

It will also suggest the shaping processes that happen during these boundaries. Comparative studies of boundaries have identified three stages. If you are in a boundary, it is easy to identify at which stage you are presently finding yourself.

This three-stage pattern is predictive in nature. You can also get a feel for what is going to happen next. The paper will suggest some attitudes and approaches for analyzing your own boundary times—whether now being experienced or already experienced in the past.

Appendix C:
About Leader Breakthru

Whether you're in a time of transition or need to move to the next level of your development as a leader, Leader Breakthru is committed to offering the best in leadership development resources to help you break through to the next level of effectiveness.

Our focus is personal clarity.

Our resources seek to facilitate breakthrough.

Our coaching and processes are all reproducible.

If you're called to make a difference, whether in the marketplace or in vocational ministry, Leader Breakthru is for you.

EXPERIENTIAL TRAINING

- Leadership Processes: Focused Living, APEX, Resonance

- Coaching Skills and Certificate training

- *Stuck!* Workshops, Band of Brothers Retreats, Life Consultations

INNOVATIVE RESOURCES

- Books, Workbooks, and PDF resources

- Online Learning Platform (Leader Breakthru University)

- GoToMeeting/Training and Cohort Learning

BREAKTHRU COACHING

- Transition Coaching

- Coach Me (personal) / Coach Us (organizational)

- Executive/Mission Coaching

For more information about the ministry of Terry Walling and Leader Breakthru, please visit: www.leaderbreakthru.com.

the leadership development series

Leader Breakthru's Leadership Development Series consists of three books that take a closer look at the three significant transition moments that every Christ-follower will face. Each of these books can be used as a personal read, a small group resource, or a one-on-one coaching resource.

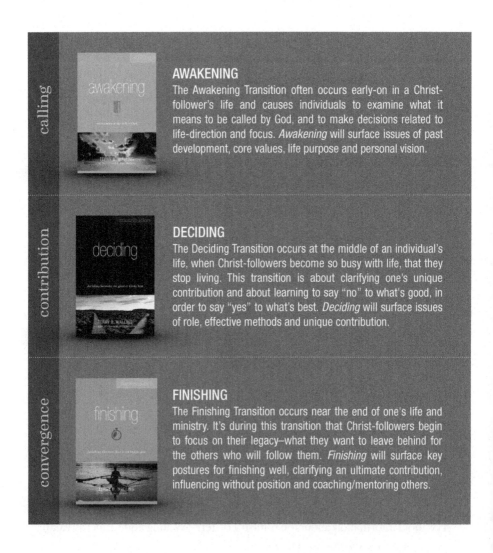

AWAKENING

The Awakening Transition often occurs early-on in a Christ-follower's life and causes individuals to examine what it means to be called by God, and to make decisions related to life-direction and focus. *Awakening* will surface issues of past development, core values, life purpose and personal vision.

DECIDING

The Deciding Transition occurs at the middle of an individual's life, when Christ-followers become so busy with life, that they stop living. This transition is about clarifying one's unique contribution and about learning to say "no" to what's good, in order to say "yes" to what's best. *Deciding* will surface issues of role, effective methods and unique contribution.

FINISHING

The Finishing Transition occurs near the end of one's life and ministry. It's during this transition that Christ-followers begin to focus on their legacy—what they want to leave behind for the others who will follow them. *Finishing* will surface key postures for finishing well, clarifying an ultimate contribution, influencing without position and coaching/mentoring others.

3 Core Processes™

Leader Breakthru offers three core, personal development processes designed to guide the ongoing development of a Christ-follower. Together, they comprise a leadership development system for churches, missions, ministries, and organizations.

If you'd like more information about these processes, would like to go through one of the processes online, or would like to gain a license to facilitate one of the processes in your context, please visit: leaderbreakthru.com.

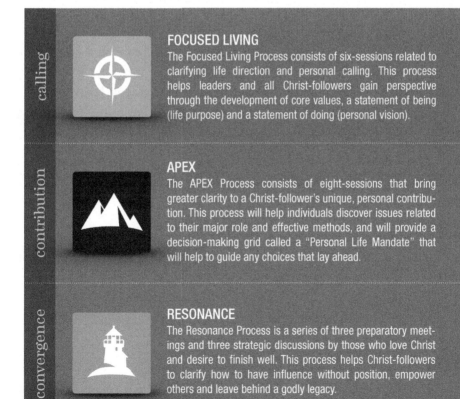

calling

FOCUSED LIVING
The Focused Living Process consists of six-sessions related to clarifying life direction and personal calling. This process helps leaders and all Christ-followers gain perspective through the development of core values, a statement of being (life purpose) and a statement of doing (personal vision).

contribution

APEX
The APEX Process consists of eight-sessions that bring greater clarity to a Christ-follower's unique, personal contribution. This process will help individuals discover issues related to their major role and effective methods, and will provide a decision-making grid called a "Personal Life Mandate" that will help to guide any choices that lay ahead.

convergence

RESONANCE
The Resonance Process is a series of three preparatory meetings and three strategic discussions by those who love Christ and desire to finish well. This process helps Christ-followers to clarify how to have influence without position, empower others and leave behind a godly legacy.

about the author

Terry Walling is President and founder of Leader Breakthru.

Terry's passion is leaders who love Christ, and lead from within. Personal renewal precedes and serves to catalyze corporate change. In order to take ministry to a new place, the leaders themselves must go to a new place.

Terry is a graduate of Point Loma College, attended Talbot Theological Seminary, and received his Doctor of Ministry from Fuller Seminary in Global Ministry and Leadership Development. Terry teaches and mentors in the Fuller Seminary's Doctor of Ministry program.

Terry has spoken and taught in a wide variety of seminaries, denominational settings, local churches, and men's retreat settings.

He and wife Robin reside in Chico, California. They have three adult, married children and Terry is grandfather of six.

Leader Breakthru focuses on coaching and resourcing breakthrough experiences for risk-taking, Kingdom leaders.

For more information about Terry B. Walling or Leader Breakthru, visit the website: www.leaderbreakthru.com

Made in the USA
Columbia, SC
09 April 2021